INVESTIGATING
CHARLES LECHMERE

INVESTIGATING CHARLES LECHMERE

WAS HE JACK THE RIPPER?

NEIL NORMAN

First published in Great Britain in 2025 by
PEN AND SWORD TRUE CRIME
An imprint of
Pen & Sword Books Ltd
Yorkshire – Philadelphia

Copyright © Neil Norman, 2025

ISBN 978 1 03610 999 8

The right of Neil Norman to be identified as Author of this work has been asserted by him in accordance with the Copyright, Designs and Patents Act 1988.

A CIP catalogue record for this book is available from the British Library.

All rights reserved. No part of this book may be reproduced, transmitted, downloaded, decompiled or reverse engineered in any form or by any means, electronic or mechanical including photocopying, recording or by any information storage and retrieval system, without permission from the Publisher in writing. NO AI TRAINING: Without in any way limiting the Author's and Publisher's exclusive rights under copyright, any use of this publication to "train" generative artificial intelligence (AI) technologies to generate text is expressly prohibited. The Author and Publisher reserve all rights to license uses of this work for generative AI training and development of machine learning language models.

Typeset in Times New Roman 12/16 by SJmagic DESIGN SERVICES, India. Printed and bound in the UK by CPI Group (UK) Ltd, Croydon, CR0 4YY.

The Publisher's authorised representative in the EU for product safety is Authorised Rep Compliance Ltd., Ground Floor, 71 Lower Baggot Street, Dublin D02 P593, Ireland.
www.arccompliance.com

For a complete list of Pen & Sword titles please contact
PEN & SWORD BOOKS LIMITED
George House, Units 12 & 13, Beevor Street, Off Pontefract Road, Barnsley, South Yorkshire, S71 1HN, England
E-mail: enquiries@pen-and-sword.co.uk
Website: www.pen-and-sword.co.uk

or

PEN AND SWORD BOOKS
1950 Lawrence Rd, Havertown, PA 19083, USA
E-mail: uspen-and-sword@casematepublishers.com
Website: www.penandswordbooks.com

Contents

Introduction vi
Chapter 1   Setting the Scene 1
Chapter 2   MDCCCLXXXVIII (1888) 5

The Canonical Five 18

Chapter 3   Mary Ann Nichols 'Polly' 19
Chapter 4   Annie Chapman 29
Chapter 5   Elizabeth Stride 38
Chapter 6   Catherine Eddowes 46
Chapter 7   Mary Jane Kelly 59
Chapter 8   The Suspects 70
Chapter 9   Why Didn't the Author of
                   Sherlock Holmes Enter the Case? 105
Chapter 10   Potential Other Ripper Victims 108
Chapter 11   Inside the Mind of the Ripper 123
Chapter 12   The Identity of the Ripper Revealed 132
Chapter 13   Completing the Puzzle 135
Chapter 14   Would Jack the Ripper Be Caught Today? 151

Bibliography 154
Other Books by Author 158
Index 159

Introduction

During the autumn of 1888, the City of London – the Jewel of the British Empire – was to make worldwide headlines, but not for a good reason; for a sadistic psychopath was roaming the East End of the city, literally carving his way into the history books. We know him by the name 'Jack the Ripper', not that his name was Jack, of course. His real name has remained elusive for more than 130 years, although many people in the past have attempted to give this fiend a true identity. Some plausible theories have been put forward, along with the absolutely bizarre, but within this book I will name the person who I truly believe to be the real Jack the Ripper.

When we go back to look at this case, we must clear our minds of all the ways in which we currently perceive police practices and even the way we conduct ourselves within society today. The late nineteenth century was a time of no forensics, no DNA, no CCTV; absolutely no technological aid at all. We must also remember the living conditions of the epoch. Things were not always as many period dramas we watch today would have you believe, and so within this book I intend to tell the real story of late Victorian London life and also policing practices, and not through rose-tinted spectacles as many have done so before.

That being said, we can, of course, use modern technology and profiling techniques to help us reach a conclusion to the case, something that is fully explored in an effort come to the conclusion as to who the *real* Jack the Ripper was…

CHAPTER 1

Setting the Scene

In 1888, London was still on a high following the previous year's pomp and circumstance due to Queen Victoria celebrating her Golden Jubilee. The 68-year-old monarch had taken the throne as a teenager and, within the following half-century, her empire had expanded to vast proportions. By the time of her Golden Jubilee, the British Empire covered 14 million square miles of territory and encompassed 450 million subjects; over 38 per cent of the world's population – very impressive given that the world's population at that time was just 1.2 billion people. It was said that the sun never set on the British Empire.

London was a manic hive of activity. Trade ships would be making their way to the capital from all corners of the world, bringing with them their precious cargos and, conversely, ships would be leaving ports to navigate their way to far-off lands and deliver their spoils. With this in mind, it is shocking to learn that one of the poorest areas of the British Empire was actually within London itself, which was so-called the 'Jewel of the Empire'.

The area of Whitechapel in the East End of London was a district that presented a breeding ground for crime, disease and poverty. The streets were covered with the filth of an overpopulated area: the smell of pollution and sewage left a pungent stench hanging in the air. Poverty and unemployment was rife, leading to many women having to resort to prostitution to provide for themselves and their families: the amount of men coming into the area on a daily basis after a long and arduous sea journey, which could take up to a few months to reach their final destination, meant that they had a regular income. The women who provided this service were known as 'unfortunates' and would literally own just the clothes on their bodies and any trinkets they had in their pockets to afford the bed they slept in each night. They spent their days and nights looking for 'punters' to earn their accommodation and basic necessities (if they were lucky).

We must also remember that no contraception was available at this time and so many bodged back-street abortions were undertaken by underqualified persons out to make quick and easy money. These procedures were often carried out in a dirty environment, which would lead to many of the women falling ill with infections or even being subjected to poisons and chemicals that ultimately would lead to an early death. Sexually transmitted diseases also led to many health problems.

The housing left much to be desired, people and families would be crammed into tight spaces with broken windows offering little protection from the elements, which allowed for houses to be damp for a great deal of the year and disease to run rampant with careless abandon. On the flip-side, the hot summer days and nights would have created an environment of stagnation beyond belief.

Although photography was in its relative infancy at the time, pictures from the period and of the area clearly show the conditions that the people lived in and the challenges people had to endure on a daily basis are very apprarant: only the strongest survived. Almost a quarter of the children born in these times went on to learn a trade, such as carpentry, butchery, or something similar. They would have grown up knowing that once they became young teenagers, their destiny was to join queues at 3.00 or 4.00 am to perhaps have a chance to do a day's work as a docker, market porter or labourer, and all for a pitiful sum of a sixpence or shilling a day, which would buy you a loaf of bread and a place to stay for the night.

The 'easier' option was to pursue a life of crime. It may be surprising to learn that stealing was not top of the list of such criminal activities, simply because there was very little worth stealing. But with assault, murder and crimes against prostitutes being commonplace, protection rackets became an affluent business whereby, for a fee each week, the local thugs would ensure that businesses didn't 'mysteriously' burn to the ground. Another way to make some quick cash was to be a police agent, or in modern day slang, a 'grass'. The police relied heavily on those who, for a modest fee, would 'sing like a canary'. These people were seen as very important in that a great amount of the crimes solved were though those with loose lips rather than actual hard work from the police – a force primarily made up of ex-servicemen from the army and navy.

Across the Channel the French were adapting to new techniques for their policing. The scene of the crime was being photographed now, and it was being cordoned off so that no evidence could be moved or destroyed. If a murder occurred in England conversely crowds would gather and in their macabre way leer at the victim, often taking away trophies from the scene of the crime as souvenirs. As soon as they left, local press reporters and police would trample over anything vital to the crime scene that could be classed as evidence.

The police were a mixed bunch of operatives. As aforementioned, the ranks were composed greatly of ex-servicemen, people who already have a degree of training and were used to following orders without hesitation. They were also able to handle themselves against the thugs and gangs that roamed the streets, after all, they were used to fighting far more established opponents than two middle-aged men bickering whilst under the influence. All this being said, there were areas where the police could only patrol in pairs for safety reasons. Some areas of an even more considered risk weren't patrolled at all.

To progress through the ranks of the force was hard to say the least. Many could become a sergeant after years of being a constable, but realistically a sergeant was nothing more than a constable, except for having more stripes on their jacket. To attain a higher rank was much harder, as these positions were filled by the upper classes (as in the case of the army). For example, the commissioner of the Metropolitan Police, Sir Charles Warren, had been a colonel in the army, and highly decorated too.

The collective Metropolitan Police force were put to the test in an event known as Bloody Sunday, which took place at Trafalgar Square, on 13 November 1887. A group of between 10,000 and 30,000 demonstrators protested about unemployment and the Irish Coercion Acts. The population of London at this time was around 5.5 million and the police numbered 14,000 (1 officer to every 393 people), and no fewer than 2,000 police were called in to halt the demonstration, along with 400 troops. Amazingly, given the calibre of weapons the demonstrators had, no reports of fatalities were recorded. Many had armed themselves with iron bars, knives, pokers and gas pipes. The official report documented 75 persons were badly injured (many of which were police), with 2 policemen being stabbed and a protester being bayoneted. Sir Charles Warren, having taken up the post of commissioner of police of the metropolis just a year earlier in 1886, was unfortunate to have this event happen on his watch (and in a Jubilee year). It was embarrassing for a man of action with a 'getting-the-job-done' ethos, but little did he know of the events that were to come in 1888 under his watch when again London would be thrown into the world headlines for all the wrong reasons.

CHAPTER 2

MDCCCLXXXVIII (1888)

A mention of the year 1888 is synonymous with one thing to most people – Jack the Ripper. But to give some context to the time, Queen Victoria was entering her 51st year as monarch and the Conservatives governed the country with its leader, Prime Minister Robert Gascoyne-Cecil 3rd Marquess of Salisbury. Some notable events of the year included the founding of the Lawn Tennis Association and the debut of the *Financial Times* going on sale. Snow fell across the country on 11 July, and the first recorded film, *Roundhay Garden Scene* was made in Roundhay, Leeds. It ran for just 2 seconds and was 18 frames in length. The Great Sheep Panic occurred in Oxfordshire when tens of thousands of sheep fled from numerous fields, John Boyd Dunlop patented his pneumatic bicycle tyre and the Lyric Theatre in London opened.

The area of Whitechapel was, as we have discussed, an area where only the bravest of outsiders would dare to venture. Flower and Dean Street was described as 'perhaps the foulest and most dangerous street in the whole metropolis'. Dorset Street earned the unsavoury title of 'the worst street in London'; Whitechapel really was the place for the social outcasts. There were 233 common lodging houses in which 8,500 people resided on a nightly basis – some 37 people per small dwelling. These houses provided cheap and basic accommodation, the nightly price for a bed was 4d (around £2 in today's money) and the less glamorous sleeping upon a 'lean-to' rope, which was stretched across the bedrooms, was 2d for adults and children alike. But for all of the 780,000 inhabitants of the area who were subjected to the daily rigours of such a brutal existence, a chain of

11 events throughout 1888 would leave the most hardened of criminals quaking in their boots, for an unseen terror was to upstage them all…

Easter Bank Holiday Monday fell on 2 April that year. It had been a cold day in London, with temperatures hovering just above 3°c. Winter had not yet relinquished its tight grip and the streets would have been clogged with the acrid smoke from many a chimney fire. That night saw temperatures fall to -3°c, but for the prostitutes of London who could not let this interfere with earning their 'doss' money or alcohol funds, they all went on their way – it was business as usual.

A 45-year-old woman named Emma Elizabeth Smith, who resided in a lodging house at 18 George Street, was unknowingly about to become famous in the annals of British crime. Not much is known about Smith's life – much of the information gathered has since been lost, stolen or destroyed over years – but it is known that she was born in 1843. The only other information we have comes via Walter Dew, who was a Metropolitan Police officer during the hunt for Jack the Ripper and would later go on to hunt for Dr Crippen before finishing his career as a detective chief inspector. He wrote the following of Smith:

> Her past was a closed book even to her intimate friends. All she had ever told anyone about herself was that she was a widow who more than ten years before had left her husband and broken away from all her early associations. There was something about Emma Smith which suggested that there had been a time when the comforts of life had not been denied her. There was a touch of culture in her speech, unusual in her class.
>
> Once when Emma was asked why she had broken away so completely from her old life she replied, a little wistfully. 'They would not understand now any more than they understood then. I must live somehow.'

At 12.15 am on 3 April, a fellow resident, Margaret Hayes, said she had seen Smith standing near Farrant Street, talking with a man dressed in dark clothes and wearing a distinct white scarf. It is believed that she was attacked at around 1.30 am at the junction of Osborn Street and Brick Lane, Whitechapel, which is located just 300 yards from the lodging house. Smith survived the attack and somehow managed to get back to the house, where she informed the deputy keeper, Mary Russell, that she had been attacked by two or three men, of which one, she stated, was a teenager. Russell and a fellow lodger, Annie Lee, then took Smith to the London Hospital where she was treated by House Surgeon George Haslip. Smith then fell into a coma and died at 9 am the following day, 4 April. Dr G.H. Hillier was charged with finding the cause of death and he discovered that Smith had had a blunt object inserted into her vagina, which had ruptured her peritoneum. An inquest was to be held on 7 April but the police were not informed until a day prior to this.

The inquest was performed by Wynne Edwin Baxter, coroner for East Middlesex, and in attendance were Russell, Hillier and John West, the chief inspector of the Metropolitan Police service. The inquest could deliver just one conclusion: a murder had been committed by a person or persons unknown. The investigation was then handed to Inspector Edmund Reid, who instantly noted the condition of Smith's clothing, saying in his report that the clothing was 'in such dirty ragged condition that it was impossible to tell if any part of it had been freshly torn'. His report was as follows:

> Emma Elizabeth Smith, 18 George Street, Spitalfields. Son and daughter living in the Finsbury Park area. She had lodged at the above address for about eighteen months, paid 4d per night for her bed. She was in the habit of leaving at about 6 or 7pm and returning at all hours, usually drunk.
>
> On the night of 2nd April, 1888, she was seen talking to a man dressed in dark clothes and white scarf, at 12.15 am (on the 3rd) she returned to her lodgings between 4 and 5 am, she had been assaulted and robbed in Osborne Street. London Hospital (near cocoa factory) Messrs, Taylor Bros. She was

attended to by Mr George Haslip, House Surgeon. She died at 9 am on the 4th. The inquest was held by Coroner Wynne Baxter at the Hospital.

The first police knew of this attack was from the Coroner's Officer who reported in the unusual manner on 6th inst, that the inquest would be held on the 7th inst, Chief Inspector West attended. None of the PCs in the area had heard or seen anything at all, and the streets were said to be quiet at the time. The offence had been committed on the pathway opposite No. 10 Brick Lane, about 300 yards from 18 George Street, and half a mile from the London Hospital to which the deceased walked. She would have passed a number of PCs en route but none was informed of the incident or asked to render assistance.

The peritoneum had been penetrated by a blunt instrument thrust up the woman's passage, and peritonitis set in which caused death. She was aged 45 years, 5'2" high, complexion fair, hair light brown, scar on right temple. No description of men.

Edmund Reid
Inspr.

This murder has remained a hot topic of debate amongst Ripperologists over the years. The fact that Walter Dew later believed it to have been carried out by the Ripper has no doubt added to its longevity but it must be remembered that the criminal gangs of the time were more than capable of delivering their own bout of justice to any prostitute who didn't tow the line. Smith was unclear if she had been attacked by two or three assailants and it's even been suggested that she had lied about the number of attackers just to cover up the fact that a single person had assaulted her. Maybe this was done to give the police no chance of finding him and thus she would face no reprisal from him when she recovered, which sadly she did not.

I am of the belief that this was an attack by a gang and was not an early Jack the Ripper case. Of course, the Ripper didn't perfect his MO immediately, but the likelihood that a gang committed the attack far outweighs that of a single person. Perhaps Emma was set upon by a group intending to rob her of her night's earnings and she had put up a fight before the assaulted her, or perhaps it was merely a gang looking to attack an unsuspecting victim that was easy prey and to not only humiliate her but also damage her person so that she could not earn any money for quite some time.

Martha Tabram

Tabram was born Martha White in Southwark, a district of central London that is situated on the south bank of the River Thames, on 10 May 1849. Her parents were Charles Samuel White, a warehouseman by trade, and his wife, Elisabeth Dowsett. Martha was the youngest of their five children and, upon maturity, had dark hair and stood 5'3" tall. Upon her 16th birthday in 1865, her parents went their separate ways, and after a brief spell of illness, Charles Tabram was to pass away in November 1865. Tabram continued to live in South London and met a foreman furniture packer named Henry Samuel Tabram. On Christmas Day 1869, aged 20, Martha and Henry were married in St Mary's Parish, Newington, which is about a mile from her birthplace. The couple moved from Newington to Southwark in early 1871 just before the birth of their first child, Frederick John Tabram, who was born in February of that year. Their second (and last) child, Charles Henry Tabram, was born in December 1872. The Tabrams' marriage was far from a settled one though and problems occurred right from the start. Martha was fond of alcohol and would drink herself into stupors so severe that she would suffer alcoholic fits, and despite the pleas from her husband and two small children, Tabram continued until her husband gave up and decided to leave her in 1875. For three years after this, he paid her the generous sum of 12 shillings a week, which would have been around half of his weekly salary. Unknown immediately to her husband, Tabram had met William Turner in 1876, a carpenter by trade and someone who found life living with her and her alcoholism equally hard. Until shortly before her death, they lived together on an on and off basis with her two children, though their official residence was at the Whitechapel Union Workhouse's casual ward at Thomas Street. In 1878, Charles Tabram learned of his former wife living with another man and quickly reduced her 12 shillings a week to a rather modest 1 shilling and sixpence. With Martha's habits remaining unchanged, it was inevitable that things between the couple would reach a breaking point eventually, and after Turner lost his job before floating in and out of employment, the couple resorted to selling trinkets and small articles on the streets. At this time they were living at Star Place, just off Commercial Road in Whitechapel in 1888. In July the couple packed up and left without notice due to owing rent, and by mid-month the pair had separated again, this time to be the last. Tabrams' final home was to be at 19 George Street, Spitalfields. At this time, she turned to prostitution to earn an income in and around Whitechapel.

A constant of the British psyche is the weather. Almost always the start of any conversation, it seems to have been ingrained in us from birth, and this must have also been the case in 1888, with that summer being a miserable one, cold and wet. The newspapers were constantly reporting on the persistent rain that fell day after day and the sun never seemed to have his 'hat on'. Bank Holiday Monday fell on 6 August and again the day was cold, overcast and dry, at least until the evening, when the skies opened. Although we will never know for sure, Tabram had probably spent what was to be her last day on Earth selling trinkets to pay for her last night. What we do know is that she met with her friend and fellow prostitute, Mary Ann Connelly, also known as 'Pearly Poll', a woman described by many tabloids as 'a tall, masculine-looking woman'. According to Connelly, in statements she changed several times after the events of that night, the two women met in a pub at 11 pm and drank there until 11.45. That being said, she told the inquest that their night together had begun at 10 pm. Martha was seen entering the White Swan pub located in the Whitechapel High Street at 11 pm by her sister-in-law, Ann Morris, who later stated that Tabram was on her own. So if this is true, Martha had met Connelly there.

Connelly said they then met two soldiers – one a corporal, the other a private – where the soldiers were more than happy to provide unlimited drinks for the next hour. At approximately midnight the four left the pub and proceeded to walk along Whitechapel High Street, where the four split into couples at the entrance to George Yard. Connelly took her soldier to an alleyway named Angel Alley, and Martha stayed at George Yard with the soldier having both passed the White Hart, a pub located next to the entrance of the yard. Being in this location was unsafe as it was well known that George Yard was one of most dangerous streets in the area. Within the yard stood a block of apartments, these were known as the George Yard Buildings and the inhabitants of these apartments were called by the *East London Observer*, 'people of the poorest description'. The outside lights were put out nightly at 11 pm and this then plunged the Yard into total darkness. Martha would most likely have frequented this area on many occasions. The events that occurred afterwards are unknown, but what we do know is that a resident of 37 George Yard Buildings, Elizabeth Mahoney, returned home at 1.40 am after an evening spent with friends. Upon arriving home, she immediately went back out to buy supper from a chandler's shop in Thrawl Street close by. She returned home five or so minutes later and noticed nothing of Tabram's body being near, where it was later found, but did concede that in the pitch black darkness she could have just walked past it. Fifteen minutes later at 2 am, PC Thomas Barrett was walking along nearby Wentworth Street, and as he passed the entrance to George Yard he saw a soldier loitering around there. Barrett spoke to him and suggested the soldier should go back to his barracks, to which the soldier replied that he was waiting for his chum who had gone off with a lady to one of the buildings. Barrett seems to have taken the soldier's word before continuing on his beat. At 3.30 am Alfred George Crow, a 21-year-old cab driver returned home to the yard. As he was walking up the stairs he noticed a person lying on the floor of the first floor landing, but paid little attention to them as he was accustomed to finding drunks passed out there on a regular basis. John Saunders Reeves headed out of his apartment on the top floor at 4.45 am to make his way to work as a casual waterside labourer. He noticed the person lying down and, because of the impending sunrise, was able to see that the body was that of a woman, lying on her back in a pool of blood. With this, Reeves rushed off to find a policeman, coming across Constable Barrett just outside the Yard. Barrett told Reeves to go and fetch Dr Timothy Killeen, a local medic, who arrived shortly afterwards. He declared the woman dead and, in his opinion, she had been brutally murdered. Brutally murdered was most certainly correct. She had received no fewer than 39 stab wounds that extended from her throat to her lower abdomen. Interestingly, Dr Killeen stated at the inquest that the injuries had been caused by two different blades, with the majority of the wounds being inflicted by a pocket knife, while the deeper wound to her breast was caused by a stronger weapon, possibly a dagger or sword bayonet. She was not known to any of the residents of George Yard so the police released the following description in the hope someone would come forth with a name.

> The body, which was that of a woman, apparently between 35 and 40 years of age, about 5ft 3in in height, complexion and hair dark, wore a dark green skirt, a brown petticoat, a long black jacket, and black bonnet. The woman is unknown to any of the occupants of the tenements on the landing on which the deceased was found, and no disturbance of any kind was heard during the night. The circumstances of the tragedy are, therefore, mysterious, and the body, which up to the time of writing, had not been identified, has been removed to Whitechapel Mortuary, and Inspector Elliston, of the Commercial Street Police Station, has placed the case in the hands of Inspector Reid, of the criminal investigation department, and that officer is now instituting inquiries.

Tabram's body was photographed at the mortuary and copies were given to policemen to take on their beats in an attempt to find out the name of their 'Jane Doe'. Of course, a potentially crucial part of the puzzle could be solved by the soldiers, especially the one Constable Barrett had spoken with at 2 am on the morning of the murder. On 7 August, Inspector Edmund Reid, who was leading the case, took Barrett to the Tower of London, where the soldiers were then based. Barrett was unable to identify the soldier he had spoken to. They returned the next day, 8 August, and the soldiers who were on leave on the Bank Holiday but had now returned were placed before Reid and Barrett. Barrett identified two men who were escorted away to be questioned privately on the premises. Upon entering the room, Barrett declared one of the men not to have been the one he had spoken to and he was dismissed. The remaining man was named John Leary. He was able to give a full account of his movements that night and this was verified by fellow soldier John Law. With this, Leary was eliminated from the enquiries. When the inquest opened on Thursday, 9 August, the identity of the woman was still unknown for sure even though it was strongly believed to be Martha Tabram. The proceeding took place at the Working Lads' Institute located at 283 Whitechapel Road. Despite evidence being given by Elizabeth Mahoney, John Saunders Reeves, Dr Killeen and Alfred George Crow, there was little point in its continuation without full proof of the deceased's identity. The only option was for the case to be adjourned for two weeks in the hope that the police could make an identification and that the killer may be caught. 'Pearly Poll' went to Commercial Street Police Station on 9 August. Here she declared that she and her friend 'Emma' had been out drinking with soldiers on the Bank Holiday Monday night. The police took her seriously: after all, the soldier link had already been followed up on, but to have a woman who had spent more time with the soldiers was a chance they could not let slip so she was asked to go to the Tower of London on the 10th. She failed to appear and the police had to track her down, which they did, before taking her to the Tower of London on Monday, 13 August. Connelly was presented with soldiers from the barracks and asked if the men who the two women had spent the night with were there, to which she shook her head. Reid then asked her, 'can you identify anyone?' 'He ain't here', was her reply. All the men were then dismissed for a second time. It was then that

Connelly had a flashback, presumably. She remembered that the soldiers they had been with had a white band around their caps, and this could only mean they belonged to the Coldstream Guards. The Coldstream Guards were stationed at the Wellington Barracks and Inspector Reid made hasty arrangements for an identity parade to be held there. The parade was to be held on Wednesday, 15 August. An account of this parade was given in the *Westminster & Pimlico News* in their edition which was published on Saturday, 18 August and read as follows:

> At noon on Wednesday there was a parade of Coldstream and Grenadier Guards at the Wellington Barracks, Pimlico. It seems that, soon after eleven o'clock two police officers – inspector Reid and detective – sergeant Caunter – arrived with Mary Ann Connelly (otherwise 'Pearly Poll') and requested permission to make certain inquiries in regard to the murder of Martha Turner, at Whitechapel on the night of the Bank Holiday. The 'assembly' call was at once sounded, and the men were drawn up in quarter – column, after which they filed through a passage, where inspector Reid, sergeant Caunter, and another police officer were stationed with 'Pearly Poll'. The woman was asked to scrutinise the faces of the soldiers as they passed, for the purpose of seeing if she could pick out either of the men who were with her and deceased on the night on which the murder was committed. After a small number had filed past, 'Pearly Poll' picked out a man wearing stripes, and taken by her to be a corporal, as the one who went away with the deceased woman.
>
>   'That's him', she exclaimed, 'I'm positive'. The suspect was temporarily detained, and the filing by the others continued. When a few more had passed, the woman, scanning the features of every one intently, pointed to a private as being the second man. She positively declared that he accompanied her to a house in the district where the murder took place.

'Are you positive?' She was asked, and 'Pearly Poll' nodded and replied, 'certain'. The military authorities immediately placed all the books, showing the time at which the suspected men left and returned to the barracks on the night mentioned, at the disposal of Inspector Reid and Sergeant Caunter. It was pointed out that the 'corporal' was but a private with good conduct stripes, a man of exemplary character, who was in the Barracks by ten o'clock on Bank Holiday night. Other evidence as to his innocence, and also respecting the private's movements on the night of the crime, was also forthcoming. The former man was at once exonerated while the second, also a man of exceptionally good character, was formally told that further inquiries must be instituted. These inquiries were duly conducted, and he too was told that no stain rested upon him, as it was clearly a case of mistaken identity,

It is asserted that as 'Pearly Poll' has 'identified' two innocent men, who could not have been in Whitechapel at the time she says, the police will not further seek her aid in elucidating the mystery. Neither of the men wore sidearms when they left the barracks on Bank Holiday, and could not possibly have been in each other's company. The authorities say that they must now look elsewhere for a clue. This clue cannot, they assert, be given by one whom they at first considered the most reliable witness.

As far as the police were concerned that was it for Connelly, she could no longer be regarded as a witness of any credibility at all. The *South Wales Echo* from Monday, 20 August certainly didn't hold back in its condemnation of 'Poll', as they reported as follows;

'Pearly Poll' is a dangerous person to trust.

She bamboozled the police into the idea that she could give them a clue to the Whitechapel murder. It was done by a corporal and a private in the Grenadier Guards at the Tower of London on Bank Holiday well, the soldiers were paraded. Poll picked out the men. But her 'corporal' was a private with two good-conduct stripes on his arm, a spotless character, and an irrefutable alibi. The other man was shown to be equally innocent, so that the police have been fooled all this time following up a false clue.

It is always dangerous to trust for identification to the evidence of an ignorant, excitable woman of 'Pearly Poll's' class – in fact, her testimony at best is never a 'Pearl of great price'.

William Turner, the man Martha had spent the past nine years with, had learned of the Whitechapel murder on the day of the initial inquest, whereupon he got in touch with police. After being taken to the local mortuary, he was able to identify the body of Martha.

Henry Tabram was to learn of his former wife's death on 13 August after hearing of the victim's name possibly being Martha as reported by the press. He contacted the police and was taken to view the body at the mortuary on 14 August, where he was able to give a positive identification.

The second inquest was to resume on the afternoon of Thursday, 23 August, given to be held at the Working Lads' Institute. Testimonies were now heard from Henry Tabram, William Turner, Mary Bousfield, Ann Morris and Mary Ann Connelly.

The deputy coroner concluded proceedings by saying that he was 'sorry that the efforts of the police to find the murderer had been fruitless so far'.

The *East London Observer* reported on 25 August that the deputy coroner also said;

> It was a most horrible crime, and showed that the deceased had been the victim of a fiend. They could only come to the conclusion that the woman had been foully and brutally murdered by some person, or persons unknown. That must be

their verdict, and the police would do what they could still do to trace the murderer.

A debate that is still hotly contested today amongst Ripperologists is was Martha Tabram a true victim of Jack the Ripper? She had been stabbed no fewer than 39 times, with her left lung being punctured 5 times, and the right 2 times. The heart (which showed signs of disease already) was punctured once and this wound was adequate to cause death. Her liver, though healthy, was stabbed in 5 places, the spleen in 2 places, and her stomach was penetrated in 6 places. These were the findings of Dr Killeen who also stated that she had been dead for 3 hours at the time of his arrival.

Although many doubt this to be a murder of the Ripper's, I am of the belief that it was indeed the first. DC Walter Dew, who was active on the case, later stated in his autobiography:

> Whatever may be said about the death of Emma Smith, there can be no doubt that the August Bank Holiday murder, which took place in George Yard Buildings… was the handiwork of the dreaded Ripper.

The savagery of the frenzied attack was, I believe, the killer's first (and successful) attempt at taking human life. He was yet to create a definitive *modus operandi* and as a result, this attack was haphazard. If Dr Killeen is to be believed, the murder occurred shortly after 2 am, and at this time the soldier who had been with 'Pearly Poll' was still waiting outside the entrance to the yard as he was approached by Constable Thomas Barrett, so the killer was very likely still hiding in the shadows at this point.

The Canonical Five

The term 'Canonical Five' was first coined by the late Jack the Ripper expert and author Martin Fido in 1987 and is used to group all five of the Whitechapel murders under one banner.

CHAPTER 3

Mary Ann Nichols 'Polly'

Mary Ann Nichols (née Walker) was born on 26 August 1845 to Edward and Caroline Walker at Dawes Court in the City of London.

Not much is known of her early life until she reached the age of 18 in 1864 when she married a man by the name of William Nichols on 16 January at St Bride's, Fleet Street. The newlyweds lived for a short time in Bouverie Street, close to Fleet Street. After this they were to move in with Mary's father at 11 Trafalgar Street, Walworth, where they would reside for a decade. In that time, they would become parents to 5 children; 3 boys and 2 girls. The next family move occurred in 1875 when they relocated to a flat in Peabody Buildings, Stamford Street, Southwark but this was not to be a happy marital home because Mary was to turn to alcohol. William was himself no saint as he had embarked on an affair with the woman who had looked after Mary after she had given birth to their last child.

As with everything in life there were two sides to the story. If you believe Mary's father, Edward, it was this affair that would lead his daughter into the depths of 'ruin'. If you believe William, however, it was purely Mary's alcoholism that set the wheels of marital decay into motion. In September 1880, however, the couple separated. William was to have full custody of two of the children, whilst the eldest, Edward, was to reside with Mary's father. Mary moved out and soon found residency at Lambeth Workhouse in South London where she would stay until the end of May 1881. During this time William paid her 5 shillings a week in maintenance allowance. He kept his ear to the ground though and it soon became apparent to him through mutual acquaintances that Mary was living with another man and that she had begun working as a prostitute, this was more than enough for him to cease his payment to her weekly. With her income from William stopped, she would make an appeal to the local parish authorities who insisted William continued to pay her but William was to counter that Mary had been the one to leave him and their children and that she now was living with another man who should be providing for them both. William was successful in his case and it was granted that Mary would no longer receive her 5 shillings a week. The two were to meet seldom thereafter, with the last meeting between them being in around 1885.

Mary was to find herself back at Lambeth Workhouse in April 1882 and she was to remain there until March the following year, when she left to resume lodgings with her father at 131 Trafalgar Street.

Her father would later state at the inquest after her death that her drinking became increasingly heavier and that this had caused numerous arguments between them. He also noted that Mary was not one to stay out late at night, although he did accept that she had spent time around a 'certain class' of females. Within eight weeks, Mary was back again at her home-from-home, Lambeth Workhouse, on 21 May 1882. She then moved to 15 York Street, Walworth, South London with Thomas Stuart Drew who was a blacksmith by trade. There was obviously still an alcohol problem that needed to be funded and she stole some items of Drew's to fuel her compulsion. Unsurprisingly, Drew disowned her and yet again she found herself moving between various workhouses until she came back to her 'beloved' Lambeth. As mentioned before, 1887 was not such a wonderful year considering the Jubilee. Many homeless people were sleeping rough in Trafalgar Square, one of which was Mary. On 23 October the Metropolitan Police commissioner, Sir Charles Warren, issued an order for the gathered masses to disband. Those who didn't heed the warning were subsequently arrested and were set to appear before the Bow Street Police Court the following morning. The media noted her as 'the worst woman in the square' and apparently in police custody she was 'very disorderly', certainly an unflattering appraisal for her.

Mary continued to live within the workhouse community and at her frequent haunt of Lambeth where she was to find friendship with a woman named Mary Ann Monk, a woman who was to later play a small part in the story. Nichols was to finally get employment as a domestic servant in the household of Samuel and Sarah Cowdry in Wandsworth. On 12 May, Mary wrote to her father to express her happiness. She seemed to have finally found her place in society, the letter was as follows:

> I just write to say you will be glad to know that I am settled in my new place, and going on all right up to now. My people went out yesterday, and have not returned, so I am left in charge. It is a grand place-inside, with trees and gardens back and front. All has been newly done up. They are teetotallers, and religious, so I ought to get on. They are very nice people, and I don't have not too much to do. I hope you are all right and the boy has work. So goodbye for the present.
>
> From yours truly,
> 'Polly'
>
> Answer soon, please, and let me know how you are.

It had been two full years since her father had heard from her and he was no doubt surprised but he replied, as requested, but she was never to see the letter.

She was clearly proud of her achievement and one would think she was destined to be content in her new role until 12 July, when a postcard from Sarah Cowdry landed on the doormat of Mary's father's home, informing him that Mary had disappeared from her job and had taken with her 3.10 shillings worth of clothing from them. So much, it seems, for her mending her ways. Mary could no longer stay in South London and so moved to East London, where she ended up finding her way to Wilmott's at 18 Thrawl Street, Spitalfields. Here she shared a room with three other women, one of which, Emily Holland, befriended her. Some three weeks later though, on 24 August, Mary had left Wilmott's and gone to another lodging house known as 'The White House' at 56 Flower and Dean Street, Spitalfields.

Thursday, 31 August dawned bright and dry. Unknown to Mary, this was to be her last day on Earth. The fine weather was not to last long though – as had been so typical of 1888, rain was to fall during the early afternoon. A heavy thunderstorm rolled over London, hours of heavy rainfall followed. Mary ended the day at the Frying Pan pub, which was located then at the junction of Thrawl Street and Brick Lane. After a few drinks she made her way back to Wilmott's to doss down for the night, and according to reports gathered later she was described as merry but certainly not drunk.

Her only mistake this evening was that she didn't have the 4d required to gain her a bed for the night. Of course, Mary Nichols is probably remembered for the 'jolly bonnet' she said she had that would – in her eyes – gain her the 4d needed for the night and as is famously known now, as she left Wilmott's she turned to the deputy keeper and told him 'I'll soon get my "doss" money. She what a jolly bonnet I've got now.' During the evening two fires broke out. One at 9 pm at a spirits warehouse in the East London Docks, which was put out just past midnight. As the exhausted crews were returning home, they were directed to a fire at Ratcliff Dry Dock. It was at this location that Mary's friend, Emily Holland, had stopped to watch the blaze along with many others. At around 2 am the fire was all but extinguished. Holland began her walk back to Wilmott's, going up Whitechapel Road. She passed St Mary's Church just as it was chiming at 2.30 am. She then crossed the road to turn into Osborn Street where she found a drunken Mary standing before her. At this point, Mary stated to her friend that she had made her doss money three times over but squandered it away. Emily tried to convince Mary to come back with her and that she would get her the bed for the night – Mary refused and insisted that she would get the money herself and told her friend, 'It won't be long before I'll be back', she drunkenly made her way into the darkness of Whitechapel Road as Emily made her way back to the lodging house. At 3.40 am a carman (driver of a horse-drawn vehicle) named Charles Allen Cross (Lechmere by birth) was making his way to work and, upon arriving at a gated stable in Buck's Row, he saw what he believed to be a tarpaulin lying on the ground. Upon inspecting it he found the tarpaulin to actually be the body of a woman laying on her back with her eyes wide open. Her legs were straight and her skirt was just above the knees. Her left hand extended out to touch the stable door. At this point Robert Paul, a fellow carman by trade, was approaching as he too made his way to work and saw Cross inspecting the woman. Cross called out to him and asked him to come over and they examined the body together. Cross touched her face, which was still warm to the touch, but her hands, upon inspection, were cold. He believed her to be dead but Paul was unsure and expressed his opinion that she may be just unconscious. Together they pulled down her skirt to give her dignity and then set about finding a policeman. Cross encountered PC Jonas Mizen at the corner of Hanbury Street and Baker's Row. He explained what the pair had discovered and told Mizen that 'she looks to me to be either dead or drunk, but for my part, I believe she's dead'. Cross and Paul then went on their journey to work, leaving Mizen at the scene. PC Mizen had not yet reached Buck's Row before another police officer, PC John Neil, approached from the opposite direction and, as he did so, his lantern illuminated the body of the woman. His lantern, in turn, grabbed the attention of another PC, John Thain. Neil shouted to Thain, 'Here's a woman with her throat cut. Run at once for Dr Llewellyn'. Thain did as he was told and left Neil to investigate the scene, looking for any evidence that had been left behind. He also noted that the street had no marks of wheels.

Dr Henry Llewellyn arrived at the scene at 4 am. He noted two deep cuts made with a knife on the woman's throat and quickly determined her to be deceased. Interestingly, he noted that her body and legs were warm and, in his opinion, she had been dead for approximately 30 minutes, PC Neil was then ordered to have the body removed and taken to the Old Montague Street Mortuary on the handcart that PC Mizen had fetched earlier. At the Old Montague Street Mortuary at 5.20 am, the wounds were discovered on her abdomen by Inspector Spratling and he immediately sent again for Dr Llewellyn, who duly arrived and re-examined the body. He discovered that she was bruised on either side of her face and that her throat wounds had been inflicted from left to right. One wound was 8 inches long and the other 4 inches long respectively. These were so deep that they reached her vertebral column. Her abdomen had one deep, jagged wound on the left side. Her vagina had been stabbed twice, and several incisions were made to the abdomen, which resulted in her bowel protruding through the wall of her stomach. The knife used was determined to have been 6–8 inches long and possibly either a cork-cutter or shoemaker knife. Each wound had been inflicted with savage force in downward thrusting motion. Although no organs were missing it is interesting to note that Dr Llewellyn was of the belief that the perpetrator of the attack had some anatomical knowledge. Another factor that surprised him was considering the wounds sustained upon the woman. Only a small amount of blood was at the scene, which was in his opinion about enough to fill two wine glasses. This led him to believe she had been facing her attacker as he placed his hand across her mouth as he then slit her throat, and these injuries would have been enough to cause death instantaneously. The mutilations to her abdomen would have been performed after death and, in Dr Llewellyn's opinion, taken five minutes to perform.

Upon her person she was carrying a white handkerchief, a comb, and a piece of glass, although her petticoats were marked 'Lambeth Workhouse P-R'. This was the workhouse that had been opened a year prior to her death and stood on Princess Road. The matron was sent for and she was unable to make an identification of the body but a resident of the workhouse, Mary Ann Monk, was called and she was able to make a positive identification – Mary Ann Nichols lay on the mortuary stab. The Working Lads' Institute on Whitechapel Road was to hold the inquest on Saturday, 1 September. Wynne Edwin Baxter, East Middlesex coroner was placed in charge. The jury were taken to view the body at the Pavilion Yard Mortuary before they returned to the institute to hear testimony from three witnesses. Nichols' father began the proceedings and stated that his daughter had been separated from her husband for 'about seven or eight years', and that he had not seen his daughter since Easter of that year. PC John Neil testified to the discovery of the body and also spoke of the circumstances he found her in. Finally, Dr Llewellyn spoke and stated the following:

> Five of the teeth were missing, and there was a slight laceration of the tongue. There was a bruise running along the lower part of the jaw on the right side of the face. That might have been caused by a blow from a fist or pressure from a thumb. There was a circular bruise on the left side of the face which also might have been inflicted by the pressure of the fingers. On the left side of the neck, about 1 inch below the jaw, there was an incision about 4 inch in length, and ran from a point immediately below the ear. On the same side, but an inch below, and commencing about 1 inch in front of it was a circular incision, which terminated at a point about 3 inch below the right jaw. That incision completely severed all the tissues down to the vertebrae. The large vessels of the neck on both sides were severed. The incision was about 8 inch in length. The cuts must have been caused by a long-bladed knife, moderately sharp, and used with great violence. No blood was found on the breast, either of the body or clothes. There were no injuries about the body until just about the lower part of the abdomen. Two or three inches from the left side was a wound running in a jagged manner. The wound was a very deep one, and the tissues were cut through. There were severed incisions running across the abdomen. There were three or four similar cuts running downwards, on the right side, all of which had been caused by a knife which had been used violently and

downwards. The injuries were from left to right and might have been done by a left-handed person. All the injuries had been (caused) by the same instrument.

The next hearing was to resume two days later on 3 September, and the first person to appear was Inspector John Spratling, who testified that he was told of the murder at 4.30 am, and at this time Nichols' body had been transferred to the mortuary. He also spoke to say that, upon questioning the people within the vicinity of the murder, he had not been able to find anyone who had either heard or seen anything. Harry Tomkins, a horse slaughterer, testified that he had not left his work after 1.00 am on 31 August and that neither he nor his colleagues had heard anything. He was asked as to the noise levels of his workhouse that night and he replied it was 'very quiet', but he did concede that he had been too far from the murder scene to have realistically heard any struggle or cries for help.

Following on were two police officers. Inspector Joseph Helson opined that the deceased had not been carried to the spot where she was found. PC Jonas Mizen testified that he was alerted to a woman lying in Buck's Row by a carman. Next to testify was Charles Cross, who spoke to confirm he had discovered the body as he was making his way to work. He stated that he believed initially that he'd stumbled upon some tarpaulin, before he realised it was actually the body of a woman. He said he next heard the footsteps of Robert Paul approaching from behind him and Cross then turned and said to Paul 'come and look over here, there is a woman lying on the pavement'. Cross said that Paul had placed his hand on the woman's heart and said, 'I think she is breathing, but very little, if she is'. Both men were now late for work and so left the woman and decided to report the body to the first policeman that they found.

Cross was also asked why neither man had noticed the wounds to the woman's throat to which he replied that Buck's Row was 'poorly illuminated'. William Nichols also testified to confirm he had not seen his wife for around three years and she had left him because of her alcoholism. Emily Holland testified to living with Mary at the same lodging house

Mary Ann Nichols 'Polly'

in the summer of 1888, she said Nichols was 'a quiet woman'. Holland also testified that she had not seen Nichols prior to their Osborn Street encounter on 31 August for around ten days. Mary Ann Monk testified to seeing Nichols entering a public house on the New Kent Road at around 7.00 pm on the evening prior to her murder. Monk also testified as to not being aware as to how Nichols earned her money.

Monday, 17 September was the opening of day three of the inquest with no fewer than eight people testifying during the day. Of note were PC John Thain who testified that this beat took him past Buck's Row every thirty minutes and that PC Neil had signalled him to the location at 3.45 am. He stated that then he was sent to fetch Dr Llewellyn and that the body was taken to the mortuary. He then testified that he searched Essex Wharf, the Great Eastern Railway arches, and the District Railway for evidence, but his searches were fruitless. The last two people to testify that day were the keeper of the Montague Street Mortuary, Robert Mann, and an inmate of the Whitechapel Workhouse named James Hatfield. Mann said he placed the body inside the mortuary at 5 am and that her clothes had not been cut in any way before he and Hatfield removed them. Hatfield later testified that both Mann and himself removed the clothing before the arrival of Dr Llewellyn. After Mann testified, the coroner adjourned all proceedings until 22 September. On that date, Coroner Baxter spoke to the panel to tell them that Nichols' body had been found where she was murdered and noted that the murderer's ability to escape into the night was he said, 'it seems astonishing, at first thought, that the culprit should have escaped detection, for there must surely have been marks of blood about his person. If, however blood was principally on his hands, the presence of so many slaughterhouses in the neighbourhood would make the frequenters of this spot familiar with bloodstained clothes and hands, and his appearance might in that way have failed to attract attention while he passed from Buck's Row in the twilight into Whitechapel Road, and was lost sight of in the mornings market traffic'.

Following a deliberation of just twenty minutes, the jury, who had been instructed to consider precisely how, when and by what means Nichols came about her death, returned a verdict of 'Wilful murder against some person or persons unknown'.

Mary Ann Nichols was laid to rest on the afternoon of 6 September 1888 at the City of London Cemetery, East London. Her body was taken there in a hearse supplied by Henry Smith, a Hanbury Street undertaker. The cortege consisted of a hearse carrying her coffin and two mourning coaches, which were occupied by her father, estranged husband, and three of her children. The streets were packed with several thousand people who observed the cortege. The coffin was polished elm and a brass plaque on it had the inscription of, 'Mary Ann Nichols, aged 42, died August 31st, 1888'. She was buried in a public grave which was numbered 210752.

The murder of Mary Ann Nichols was certainly a ferocious one. If we consider that Martha Tabram was indeed the first true victim, we can see clearly that the attack on Nichols certainly showed a dramatic increase in the murderer's methods and brutality. The murderer at this point would no doubt be confident that he could kill at will, with ease, and he most certainly knew his surroundings like the back of his hands. It's fair to say he must also have had a knowledge of the police patrol times. Within days his urge and bloodlust would be shown to all again.

Chapter 4

Annie Chapman

Annie Chapman was born Eliza Ann Smith in Paddington on 25 September 1840. Her father, George, was a soldier in the 2nd Regiment of Life Guards and Chapman's early life revolved around her father's service between London and Windsor. In 1844 the family moved to Knightsbridge where her father became a valet. The family moved again in 1856, this time to Berkshire. The 1861 census states that the Smith family were then living in Clewer, near Windsor, but Annie was not living there. Instead she was still in London and working as a domestic servant. In 1863, her father committed suicide by cutting his throat. Even from an early age, Annie was drawn to alcohol, her particular favourite being rum. She was just 5 feet tall with blue eyes and dark brown, wavy hair, her friends gave her the nickname of 'Dark Annie'.

Annie married John James Chapman on 1 May 1869. They were married at All Saints Church in Knightsbridge with the witnesses being Emily Laticia, Annie's sister, and George White, a work colleague of John's. The marital home is given on the marriage certificate as 29 Montpelier Place, Brompton. The couple had three children, with Emily Ruth being born 25 June 1870, followed by Annie Georgina on 5 June 1873, and finally John Alfred on 21 November 1880. Sadly, John was born crippled and medical help was sought for him at a London hospital before they later placed him in the care of an institution for the physically disabled close to Windsor. Tragically, this was the event that caused Annie to turn to drink again as it is said that by 1880, she had all but stopped drinking. Further tragedy would strike when Emily Ruth died of meningitis on her brother's 2nd birthday, she was aged just 12. Both parents, grief-stricken to the core, turned to alcohol to try and repair the damage done to them by fate's cruel hand but by 1884, they could take it no more and decided to separate. John retained custody of their surviving daughter and he was to pay her 10 shillings a week. John was to die on Christmas Day 1886 due to liver cirrhosis and edema, which meant Annie would lose the income she had depended upon greatly, although at the time she was living in Whitechapel with a man who made wire sieves for a living. The man left Annie shortly after her allowance ceased and moved away to Notting Hill. This made Annie depressed, with a friend of hers noting that this event made Annie seem to lose the will to live. During late spring and early summer, Chapman was residing at 35 Dorset Street in Crossingham's Lodging House. There she was spending 8 pence a night for a double bed which, by all accounts, was occupied by a bricklayer's labourer named Edward 'The Pensioner' Stanley from Saturday to Monday who would occasionally pay for her bed. Chapman earned a living by selling flowers, crochet work, making antimacassar and casual prostitution. Chapman and a fellow lodger, Eliza Cooper, fought eight days before Chapman's death over a trader named Harry who they both shared affections for, though later Cooper insisted they had fought over a bar of soap and that upon being asked to return it, Chapman simply threw a halfpenny on to the kitchen table, stating, 'go get a halfpenny's worth of soap'. The fight that took place at the Britannia pub resulted in Chapman being hit in the face and chest by Cooper, leading to a bruised breast and black eye.

Amelia Palmer was to encounter Chapman on 7 September in Dorset Street; she would later say that Chapman appeared pale and had told her that she was 'too ill to do anything'. Chapman had been released early that day from the Whitechapel Infirmary. An interesting note here is that her days were quite literally numbered as the coroner at her autopsy noted that her lung and brain membranes were in an advanced state of disease, and that she would have died within months regardless.

Just after midnight on 8 September, the lodging house deputy, Timothy Donovan, and the watchman, John Evans, asked Annie for her evening's doss money but since she was unable to pay she sat in the kitchen with fellow lodger Frederick Stevens and drunk a pint of beer at 12.10 am and apparently told another lodger that she had earlier that day visited her family in Vauxhall, who had given her 5d. Stevens then saw Chapman take a box of pills from her pocket. The box broke and the pills within fell out, Chapman gathered up the pills and wrapped them within a piece of envelope that she had obtained from the lodgings' mantlepiece before she exited the premises. As she left she said, 'I won't be long, Brummie, see that Tim keeps the bed for me'. She then made her way off towards Spitalfields Market. At 5.30 am Chapman was observed talking to a man just beyond the backyard of 29 Hanbury Street by a Mrs Elizabeth Long. Long described the man as being over 40 years old, slightly taller than Chapman, with dark hair, and of a foreign, 'shabby-genteel' appearance. He was wearing a brown low-crowned felt hat and possibly a dark coat. Long also stated that the man asked Chapman, 'will you?' to which she replied, 'yes'. If Long indeed was correct with her sighting of Chapman at 5.30 am (she stated she'd heard a striking of a nearby clock) then it's almost certain the man with her at that time was her murderer. At around 5 am, John Richardson, the son of a resident at 29 Hanbury Street, entered the backyard of the dwelling to check the padlocked cellar and to also trim some leather from his boot. Richardson observed the cellar to still be locked before he sat upon the step to trim his boot. He then left the premises via the front door, after spending around three minutes there. Some ten minutes later at around 5.15 am, Albert Cadosch who lived at 27 Hanbury Street entered into the yard to use the privy. At this point, he later said he heard a woman say, 'no, no!' before hearing the sound of something (or someone) falling against the fence that was between numbers 27 and 29 Hanbury Street. Either thinking no more of it or just not being brave enough to investigate, he went back inside number 27. It was to be just forty-five minutes later at 6.00 am that the body of Chapman was discovered by John Davis, a resident of number 29. He saw that the front door was now open while the back was closed. Chapman's body lay on the ground close to the doorway to the backyard. In panic, Davis alerted three men by the names of Henry Holland, James Kent and James Green, and the three promptly ran down Commercial Street in a bid to find the nearest policeman whilst Davis went to the nearest police station to report his find. Inspector Joseph Luniss Chandler was not far from the scene on the corner of Hanbury Street when the three men approached him and told him that a woman had been murdered. Chandler followed the men back the short distance to Chapman's lifeless body. Upon seeing the body, Chandler immediately called for police surgeon Dr George Bagster Phillips and more officers. Within a few minutes, back up arrived and Dr Phillips appeared at around 6.30 am. He quickly noted the similarities with the murder of Mary Ann Nichols just eight days prior. Chapman was found lying on her back with her legs bent at her knees with her dress above the knees. Her right arm was at her side, and her left covered her left breast. Her small intestines that were attached by a cord, along with part of her abdomen were situated above her right shoulder; two flaps of skin from the abdominal area lay in a large pool of blood above the left shoulder. The throat was deeply cut in a jagged manner, her face was swollen and turned to her right side. The tongue swollen and protruded between her front teeth. Rigor mortis had not yet set in but was in the process of setting in. The body was cold but some heat was felt under her intestines. Dr Phillips concluded that the wounds inflicted were carried out by a knife like that used on Nichols. He also noted six areas of blood splatter against the walls of the house and some splatter was 18 inches high.

Within close proximity to the lifeless body of Chapman were two pills (which she was taking for a lung condition), a small piece of torn muslin, the shred of envelope used to wrap the tablets in and a leather apron near the body that was in a bowl of water.

Wynne Edwin Baxter was put in charge of the inquest into Annie Chapman's murder, which opened on 10 September at the Working Lads' Institute. The opening day saw the jury hear testimonies from four witnesses. John Davis testified to discovering the body and also that he had lived at Hanbury Street for just two weeks. Timothy Donovan and

John Edwards testified to having made an identification of the deceased. Donovan also stated he'd last seen Chapham at 1.50 am on the 8th and her final words to him had been, 'I have not sufficient money for my bed. Don't let it. I shan't be long before I am in.' Amelia Palmer appeared to give a character testimony of Chapman by saying she'd known the deceased for many years and stated that, although fond of an alcoholic drink, Chapman was a respectable woman who was not in the habit of using profanity in her language, she also went on to say that Chapman had 'not as a regular means of livelihood' been working as a prostitute, and that she made most of her money by making and selling crochet work; prostitution had only become a means to an end after her husband had died two years prior, on Christmas Day 1886. Timothy Donovan testified that Chapmam had been a good lodger at the house and that her altercation with Eliza Cooper on 31 August had been the only time Chapman had been involved in trouble. He also stated that she would only be the worst for drinking on a Saturday night as a rule and that the rest of the week she was sober. The second day saw testimonies from the residents of Hanbury Street with notably that of John Richardson, who testified that the passageway through the house to the backyard was not locked and it was common for people to loiter around the area at all times of the day. The third day of the inquest was reserved for the medical and police reports. Dr George Bagster Phillips was to describe how he had seen the body when he arrived on the scene at 6.30 am at 29 Hanbury Street.

> The left arm was placed across the left breast. The legs were drawn up, the feet resting on the ground, and the knees turned outwards. The face was swollen and turned on the right side. The tongue protruded between the front teeth, but not beyond the lips. The tongue was evidently much swollen. The front teeth were perfect as far as the first molar, top and bottom and very fine teeth they were. The body was terribly mutilated... the stiffness of the limbs was not marked but was evidently commencing. He noticed that the throat was dissevered deeply,

that the incisions through the skin were jagged and reached right round the neck… On the wooden paling between the yard in question and the next, smears of blood, corresponding to where the head of the deceased lay, were to be seen. These were about 14 inches from the ground, and immediately above the past where the blood from the neck lay… The instrument used at the throat and abdomen was the same. It must have been a very sharp knife with a thin narrow blade and must have been at least 6 to 8 inches in length, probably longer. He should say that the injuries could not have been inflicted by a bayonet or a sword bayonet. They could have been done by such an instrument as a medical man used for post mortem purposes, but the ordinary surgical cases might not contain such an instrument. Those used by the slaughtermen, well ground down, might have caused them. He thought the knives used by those in the leather trade would not be long enough in the blade. There were indications of anatomical knowledge… he should say that the deceased had been dead at least two hours, and probably more when he first saw her but it was right to mention that it was a fairly cool morning and that the body would be more apt to cool rapidly from its having lost a great quantity of blood. There was no evidence… of a struggle having taken place. He was positive the deceased entered the yard alive… A handkerchief was round the throat of the deceased when he saw it early in the morning. He should say it was not tied on after the throat was cut.

The murderer had acted in pure cold-blooded barbaric ferocity. Chapman's throat had been slashed from left to right all the way down to her vertebral column. Some flesh lay across her left shoulder as she had also been subjected to disembowelment, and her small intestines had been placed over her right shoulder. She was later found to be missing part of her uterus and bladder. The handkerchief around her neck was believed by

Dr Phillips to have been used to asphyxiate her before the murderer slashed her throat, and it was also concluded by the doctor that she had been killed where she was found as there was no blood trail leading to the body. Interestingly, he concluded that Chapman was sober at the time of her death and hadn't drunk any alcohol for several hours leading up to her death. He was the first person to spawn the idea that the murderer had anatomical knowledge as he had cut out her uterus with a single motion. This has been called into doubt in the years following and a suggestion has been made that this may have been performed by staff at the mortuary as a practice of selling organs as medical specimens was common practice. Even the coroner made a suggestion that Chapman had been murdered so that her organs could be sold to an American who was alleged to have been interested in obtaining the organs. This was later to be proven to be erroneous and the theory was dropped thereafter.

Another point of interest was that Dr Phillips stated he'd believed Chapman to have been killed at around 4.30 am, going against what all the eyewitnesses had testified to. This can be explained by bad timekeeping on the eyewitnesses' part, but the timing of death had certainly not yet become an accurate science either. The inquest lasted a full five days. Upon the last day, which had been adjourned to 26 September, no further persons were called to testify. Before being sent away to deliberate their conclusion, Coroner Baxter turned to them and said, 'I have no doubt that if the perpetrator of this foul murder is eventually discovered, our efforts will not have been useless.' As with the Nichols case before, the jury returned a verdict of wilful murder against a person or persons unknown.

The leather apron near the body of Chapman (which later became an item of folklore) belonged to John Richardson and was placed there two days prior on 6 September by his mother who had washed it. Richardson was fully investigated and eliminated quickly but once the press had gotten hold of the news about the apron it was to set the press on fire. Much speculation was created simply because very little in the way of facts and details of the crimes was being given to them by the police and so, in true media style, they created their own version of events to fills the gaps. The public were growing increasingly anxious and curious and the media bosses saw a way to sell their papers with careless abandon. With a great deal of the Whitechapel population being Polish immigrants, Jewish stereotypes began to appear in the press, and a character called 'leather apron' was created. Unfortunately, a man named John Pizer, a 38-year-old Polish Jew was locally known as 'Leather Apron' because his trade was making leather footwear. He also had a questionable character in that he would intimidate prostitutes at knifepoint. He had, in fact, only recently appeared before the Thames Magistrates' Court on 4 August, being charged with indecent assault and it is said that in 1887, he had stabbed a man in the hand. With this knowledge of his reputation but with no firm evidence against him, Sergeant William Thicke arrested Pizer on 10 September. He was to be released from custody the next day after his alibis were verified for both nights of the Nichols and Chapman murders. He also appeared at the second day of Chapman's inquest to clear his name and was successful in claiming financial compensation from at least one of the tabloids that had named him as the main suspect in the murders. Several other suspects were questioned or arrested but no substantial evidence could be gathered against them and all were released. Chapman was buried just after 9.00 am on 14 September 1888 in a communal grave inside Manor Park Cemetery, Forest Gate, East London. The service was paid for by her family and, at their request, the funeral was not publicised. Only relatives attended the ceremony. Her body was placed in an elm coffin and draped in black at the Whitechapel Mortuary in Montague Street at 7.00 am before being taken to Spitalfields undertaker Harry Hawes, who had arranged the funeral. The plate upon the coffin was inscribed 'Annie Chapman, died Sept 8, 1888, aged 48 years'. Today the precise location of the grave is unknown but a plaque was placed there in 2008 and reads, 'Her remains are buried within this area'.

Just under a fortnight later on 27 September, a letter addressed to the Central News Agency arrived. This was no ordinary letter as it was believed to have been known as the 'Dear Boss' letter. It reads as follows:

Annie Chapman

Dear Boss,

I keep on hearing the police have caught me but they wont fix me just yet. I have laughed when they look so clever and talk about being on the right track. That joke about Leather Apron gave me real fits. I am down on whores and I shant quit ripping them till I do get buckled. Grand work the last job was. I gave the lady no time to squeal. How can they catch me now. I love my work and want to start again. You will soon hear of me with my funny little games. I saved some of the proper red stuff in a ginger beer bottle over the last job to write with but it went thick like glue and I cant use it. Red ink is fit enough I hope ha, ha. The next job I do I shall clip the ladys ear off and send to the police officers just for jolly wouldn't you keep this letter back till I do a bit more work, then give it out straight. My knife's so nice and sharp I want to get to work right away if I get a chance.

Good Luck.

Yours truly
Jack the Ripper

Dont mind me giving the trade name.
PS: Wasnt good enough to post this before I got all the red ink off my hands curse it No Luck yet. They say I'm a doctor now. Ha ha.

The letter was forwarded on to Scotland Yard on 29 September and was believed to have been a hoax. Much conjecture about the letter has followed over the decades and it is widely thought today that this was written by a journalist. Some regard it as a stroke of genius because the Whitechapel murderer now had a name – Jack the Ripper had been born.

CHAPTER 5

Elizabeth Stride

Elizabeth Gustafsdotter was born on 27 November 1843 in Stora Tumlehed, Torslanda, a small town and parish located to the west of Gothenbury, Sweden. She was the second of four children and grew up on a farm and was raised in the Lutheran faith. At the age of 15 she relocated to the city of Gothenburg where she sought employment and eventually gained a post as a domestic worker for the Olofsson family, where she worked until 2 February 1864. She left this post to move across the city where she again found employment as a domestic servant, this time only staying there for two years before she decided to move to London. The exact reason for this move is unknown as Gustafsdotter gave two reasons for the change of location. One of the stories she told was that she moved to be a domestic servant to 'a gentleman' who resided near Hyde Park, whilst another of her stories was that she had family in London. In any event, she eventually decided to stay in the country, probably using the 65 Krona she inherited upon her mother's death in 1864 but received in late 1865. Gustafsdotter was between 5 feet 2 inches, and 5 feet 5 inches tall, with curly dark brown hair, light grey eyes and a pale complexion. She was also obviously intelligent because upon arriving in England she learned to speak both English and Yiddish and, as an irony, she had once dated a policeman in the late 1860s. Gustafsdotter did eventually meet a man named John Thomas Stride who was employed as a ship's carpenter and 22 years her senior. They married on 7 March 1869 at a small service at St Giles in the Fields church. The couple were to have no children. After the marriage, the couple lived in East India Dock Road where they ran a coffee shop in Poplar, East London. John was also continuing to work as a carpenter. The marriage began to fail by 1874 and in 1875 John sold the coffee shop, most likely due to financial reasons. Things after this date become a little messy for in March 1877, Stride was at Poplar Workhouse which indicates that the couple were no longer together but records of the 1881 census show that the two were together and living in the district of Bow within the London borough of Tower Hamlets. It appears the couple had separated completely by the end of 1881 where Stride was in the Whitechapel Workhouse infirmary with bronchitis where she spent a month before being released on 4 January 1882 where she took up residence in several lodging homes on Flower and Dean Street, located in Whitechapel. Her former husband was to pass away in 1884 from tuberculosis. The following years would see Stride tell a story that her husband and two of her nine children died during the sinking of SS *Princess Alice*, a paddle steamer that sank on 3 September 1878 after a collision with collier SS *Bywell Castle* on the River Thames, resulting in 600–700 deaths. She claimed that she had climbed the mast but while doing so she was kicked in the mouth with the injury causing her to have a permanent stutter. After this, Stride lived with a dock labourer named Michael Kidney in Devonshire Street. By all accounts the couple had an on-off relationship and with this, Stride would often again find herself in lodging houses. An indication of the relationship was that in April 1887, Stride made an assault charge complaint against Kidney but later failed to follow it through. Stride was noted for her good nature but it seems that once she had had a few too many drinks, she could become quite a feisty lady; she was especially familiar with the Thames Magistrates' Court where she would grace them with her presence no fewer than eight times for a combination of drunk and disorderly offences and foul language.

Shortly before her death, Stride and Kidney separated for one last time. On 26 September she then sought lodgings at 32 Flower and Dean Street, which was known locally as a place where criminals frequented, but by all accounts, she behaved and earned money by performing cleaning duties for the locals of the area and even at her lodging house on 29 September, for which she was paid a sixpence. It is known that Stride and the housekeeper at 32 Flower and Dean Street, Elizabeth Tanner, visited the Queen's Head pub located on Commercial Street before Stride returned home by herself. However, it was later claimed by eyewitnesses that Stride had actually spent time later that evening in the company of men. One of these men was described as being short with a dark moustache and wearing a morning suit with a bowler hat, this was approximately 11.00 pm near Berner Street. At 11.45 pm Stride was seen by a labourer named William Marshall as she stood on the pavement opposite 58 Berner Street. Marshall said the man seen with Stride wore a peaked cap, a black coat and dark trousers. Marshall also noted that the two kissed and that he heard the man say to her 'You would say anything but your prayers'. On 30 September at 12.35 am Stride was seen by PC William Smith talking to a man who was wearing a hard felt hat, this time outside the International Working Men's Educational Club located at 40 Berner Street. Of interest is that Smith noted the man was carrying a package that was around 18 inches long. A dockworker named James Brown saw a woman he thought to be Stride standing on the corner of Berner Street with her back against a wall at around 12.45 am, and again Stride was talking with a man. This time he was said to be wearing a long black coat and was of average build and, according to Brown, he heard Stride say to the man 'No, not tonight some other night'. Elizabeth Stride's body was discovered just 15 minutes later at 1.00 am within Dutfield's Yard by Louis Diemschutz, who was the steward of the International Working Men's Educational Club. He had driven his two-wheeled cart into the dimly lit yard before his horse shied to the left to avoid a bundle lying on the ground. Diemschutz then tried to move the object with his whip but was unsuccessful so he then stepped down from his cart to make a closer inspection of the bundle. He lit a match, and the small amount of light offered by the match revealed that the bundle was, in fact, the body of a woman. He ran to the club to check that his wife was safe. This confirmed, he told the people gathered inside of his grizzly find, and the group then promptly sought help. The body had a single knife wound that blood was still flowing from and it was found that areas of her body were cold to the touch whilst others were warm, but her hands were cold. This is an indication that she had been murdered shortly before Diemschutz had found her. Oddly, several people leaving the club between 12.30 am and 12.50 am reported seeing absolutely nothing. The first doctor on scene was Frederick William Blackwell and he was followed shortly after by Dr George Bagster Phillips, who had examined Annie Chapman. Dr Phillips' post mortem report read as follows:

> The body was lying on the near side, with the face turned toward the wall, the head up the yard and the feet toward the street. The left arm was extended and there was a packet of cachous in the left hand…. The right arm was over the belly, the back of the hand and wrist had on it clotted blood. The legs were drawn up with the feet close to the wall. The body and face were warm and the hand cold. The legs were quite warm. The deceased had a silk handkerchief round her neck, and it appeared to be slightly torn. I have since ascertained it was cut. This corresponded with the right angle of the jaw. The throat was deeply gashed, and there was an abrasion of the skin about one and a quarter inches in diameter, apparently stained with blood, under her right brow.
>
> At 3 pm on Monday at St. George's Mortuary, Dr Blackwell and I made a post-mortem examination rigor mortis was still thoroughly marked. There was mud on the left side of the face and it was matted in the head… The body was fairly nourished. Over both shoulders, especially the right, and under the collarbone and in front of the chest there was a blueish discolouration, which I have watched and have seen on two occasions since. There was a clear-cut incision on the neck. It was six inches in length and commenced two and a half inches in a straight line below the angle of the jaw, three-quarters of an inch over an undivided muscle, and then, becoming deeper,

dividing the sheath. The cut was very clean and deviated a little downwards. The arteries and other vessels contained in the sheath were all cut through. The cut through the tissues on the right side was more superficial and tailed off to about two inches below the right angle of the jaw. The deep vessels on that side were uninjured. From this, it was evident that the hemorrhage was caused through the partial severance of the left carotid artery and a small bladed knife could have been used. Decomposition had commenced in the skin. Dark brown spots were on the anterior surface of the left chin. There was a deformity in the bones of the right leg, which was not straight but bowed forwards. There was no recent external injury save to the neck. The body is being washed more thoroughly. I could see some healing sores. The lobe of the left ear was torn as if from the removal or wearing through of an earring, but it was thoroughly healed. On removing the scalp there was no sign of bruising or extravasation of blood… The heart was small, the left ventricle firmly contracted, and the right slightly so. There was no clot in the pulmonary artery, but the right ventricle was full of dark clot. The left was firmly contracted as to be absolutely empty. The stomach was large and the mucous membrane only congested. It contained partly digested food, apparently consisting of cheese, potato, and farinaceous powder (flour or milled grain). All the teeth on the lower left jaw were absent.

With such a detained report given, Dr Blackwell was of the opinion that Stride had been pulled backwards onto the ground by the murderer, pulling at her neckerchief before going on to cut her throat. Phillips backed this up and added he also believed that Stride had most likely been on her back when a single, swift slash wound from left to right across her neck which indicated the murderer was right handed. The bruising she sustained on her chest indicated that she had been pinned down before the neck wound was carried out. It is at this point that one of the most notable figures of the case appears – Israel Schwartz. He informed police that he had seen Stride being attacked at around 12.45 am by a man he described as being 5 feet 5 inches tall, dark hair and with a small brown moustache. Schwartz would also say that the man with Stride attempted to pull her onto the street before then turning her around and pushing her to the ground. Apparently the man then shouted out the word 'Lipski' (a derogatory term referring to a man named Israel Lipski, who had been convicted and hung for murder in August 1887) Schwartz fearing an altercation then ran off. A Mrs Fanny Mortimer, who lived two doors away from the club, was listening to the communal singing around the time of Stride's death but had not witnessed anyone or heard anything. She did, however, see a man racing past but the individual was later identified as Leon Goldstein and no further police inquiry was pursued. The investigation certainly reached out to the community as by 19 October, no fewer than 2,000 lodgers had been questioned and at least 80,000 leaflets asking for information regarding the murder had been distributed in and around the area of Whitechapel.

On 1 October, the inquest was opened at the Vestry Hall, Cable Street, St George in the East. Again the Middlesex coroner, Wynne Edwin Baxter, was placed in charge. The first day was to hear testimonies from three people, two who had been at the International Working Men's Educational Club, and also from Louis Diemschutz. The witnesses from the club, named William Wess and Morris Eagle, spoke to confirm that there had been between 25-30 people in attendance at the club that night when the body of Stride was found and that nothing relating to the murder had been heard by anyone. Wess spoke also to state that he had left the club at around 12.15 am and the body of Stride was not in the location it was found at that time. Diemschutz was to speak and say how he'd discovered the body and also to confirm it had taken around twenty minutes for the doctor to arrive on scene after the police had been alerted. Day two began as a debacle. It was stated that the deceased may not actually be Stride at all. Mrs Mary Malcolm was adamant the woman was her sister, Elizabeth Watts, but the police were sure they knew the identity of the dead woman with certainty. Frederick Blackwell, doctor and surgeon, stated that he attended the scene at 1.16 am and was joined twenty minutes later by Dr Phillips. Blackwell also spoke to confirm that blood from the slash to her throat was still flowing when he arrived, and that it was flowing into a gutter and down into a drain close to her feet. In addition, he stated that death had occurred between 20-30 minutes before his arrival. The cut to her throat was on one side, meaning that as her carotid artery was only severed partially, she would have died 'comparatively slowly' and would not have been able to cry out for help. Character testimonies began on 3 October. Firstly, Elizabeth Tanner from the lodging house spoke, to say she had known Stride for around six years as she'd lodged on and off at 32 Flower and Dean Street but had been away from the house for three months before 26 September. She stated that Stride was a quiet and sober woman, and that although she was a Swedish native, her English was as good as that of any English woman. She also retold the story of how Stride had informed her that her husband and children had drowned in the 1878 SS *Princess Alice* paddle steamer sinking. Catherine Lane, a charwoman, spoke to also confirm she had known Stride for around six months and that Stride had told her she had fallen out with her partner and that was her reason for now residing at the lodging home at Flower and Dean Street. Stride's partner, Michael Kidney, also appeared on 3 October and confirmed that the two had been in a relationship for the past three years and that they had separated on numerous occasions but that she always came back to him. He stated that her heavy drinking was a major factor in their turbulent relationship. The inquest was to last five days, with the final day being 23 October. Coroner Baxter gave his findings on the murder, saying he believed her to have been attacked in a quick manner and that her death was, without question, murder, as there were no indicators or any circumstance that could reduce it to manslaughter. He also agreed with the previous thoughts of Dr Phillips that the murderer took full advantage of the checked scarf Stride wore to grab her from behind before slitting her throat. Adding that the absence of a shout for assistance and the lack of obvious marks of a struggle indicated that Stride had willingly laid down on the ground before the murderer inflicted the fatal wound to her throat. The fact that Stride was holding a packet of cachous in her left hand showed clearly that she didn't have time to act in self defence, in his opinion. As before, the jury had been instructed to deliberate precisely how, when, and by what means Stride came about her death. They returned a unanimous verdict: 'Wilful murder against some person or persons unknown'. As with the previous murders it was believed that this was the work of the Ripper, but one fact left many wondering, even today: Stride only suffered the cut to her throat, and no abdominal mutilations were performed. This led some to believe Stride's attack to be one performed by a disgruntled 'punter', but the fact was her death had incorporated the slashing of her throat, which sat well within the MO from the previous victims, and thus the police added Stride to the Whitechapel list of murders. It is interesting to note that her death was the only Ripper murder to occur south of Whitechapel Road, and it is believed that the knife used was of a different design and shorter in length than the one used in previous attacks. Many believe that the attacker didn't go on to mutilate the body of Stride because he heard Diemschutz approaching and so retreated back into Dutfield's Yard, before escaping after Diemschutz went to the club.

Elizabeth Stride was laid to rest on Saturday, 6 October in East London Cemetery at Plaistow. Only a small number of mourners attended and her gravestone is still visible today and simply inscribed 'Elizabeth Stride 1843–1888'.

CHAPTER 6

Catherine Eddowes

Catherine Eddowes was born on 14 April 1842 in Graiseley Green, Wolverhampton. She was the sixth of twelve children born to George and Catherine Eddowes. George relocated his family to London in 1843 where he took a job with a company named Perkins and Sharpus in Bell Court. Their first residence was at 4 Baden Place in Bermondsey before settling at 35 West Street. Eddowes' mother, Catherine, died of tuberculosis aged 42 in 1855. Within the next two years her father had died too, leaving 15-year-old Catherine and her siblings orphans. Eddowes and three of her siblings were admitted at Bermondsey workhouse and were educated at a local industrial school in an aim to give them all a trade. Eventually Eddowes secured her first job as a tinplate stamper at the Old Hall Works in Wolverhampton. Eddowes moved back and lived with her aunt whilst continuing her education at Downgate Charity School. Employment wasn't to last long, however, as Eddowes was sacked from her job for being caught stealing. This in turn caused tensions between her and her aunt and shortly after she moved to Birmingham where she took residence with her uncle, Thomas Eddowes. She quickly found employment there as a tray polisher within a firm in Legge Street, Birmingham. This was to be a brief four months before she moved back to Wolverhampton where she lived with her grandfather who secured her a job as a tinplate stamper.

Following this, she moved back to Birmingham, where she met Thomas Conway, who had been a soldier in the 18th Royal Irish Regiment. They were to have two children: Catherine Ann 'Annie' born in 1863, and Thomas Lawrence, born in 1867. Conway had poor health but took labouring jobs when he could to support his family. It is unclear if the two were married but it is known that Eddowes would refer to herself as 'Kate Conway' and that she had his initials crudely tattooed in blue ink on her forearm. Eddowes and Conway decided to move to London in 1868 and lived in Westminster. Five years later, in 1873, Eddowes gave birth to their third child, but it was at this time that Eddowes began drinking. This would cause many arguments with her family, especially as Eddowes was known to have a fierce temper. In fact, during the later inquest into her mother's death, Catherine 'Annie' Phillips stated that her parents started living on 'bad terms' because of her mother's drinking, which would get far worse during the 1870s. Her father was a teetotaller and found Eddowes to be impossible to live with and the arguments only increased and intensified, resulting in violence to the point where Eddowes would be seen out and about with black eyes and bruising on her face. The pair were residing at 71 Lower George Street in Chelsea with their two youngest children (Catherine had left the household by this time) and this was to be the year that the pair would separate. Within a year, Eddowes had left Chelsea and moved to the East End and was living with a new partner named John Kelly, who earned a living as a fruit salesman, and the pair resided at 55 Flower and Dean Street, Spitalfields. It was here she was known locally as 'Kate Kelly', and where she worked as a domestic servant within the Jewish community on Brick Lane. It is also suspected that she took up prostitution to pay the daily rent. Eddowes and Kelly earned money also by hop picking in Kent each summer from 1885 onwards. It is known that when Eddowes was struggling for income she would often try to borrow money from her sisters or her daughter, with her eldest sister, Elizabeth Fisher, who lived in Greenwich, being favoured. When she failed to gather money for her nightly doss, she is believed to have slept rough in the front room of 26 Dorset Street.

In the September of 1888, Eddowes and Kelly had, as usual, travelled to the small village of Hunton, Kent, to work as hop pickers. It is known that Eddowes had bought a jacket from a pawnshop and that Kelly had purchased a pair of boots from Maidstone. Upon arriving in Hunton, the pair befriended a woman named Emily Birrell and her common-law husband.

After the hop picking was complete, all four returned to London with Birrell and her common-law husband parting midway as they intended travelling on to Cheltenham. Just prior to separating, Birrell handed Eddowes a pawn ticket and said, 'I have got a pawn ticket for a flannel shirt. I wish you'd take it since you're going (to London). It is only for 9d, and it may fit your old man'. Eddowes gladly took it and placed it within a small mustard tin she carried. Eddowes and Kelly arrived back in London on 27 September. The following night saw them separated and they slept in separate lodging houses, with Eddowes bedding down at the Mile End Casual Ward and Kelly sleeping at 52 Flower and Dean Street. It is reported that Eddowes was asked by the superintendent of the casual ward where she'd recently been, to which Eddowes responded by saying she'd been hop picking in Kent before adding that she would be soon collecting the reward for the Whitechapel murderer as she knew his identity. On 29 September, Eddowes and Kelly had all but spent the money they had earned hop picking and were down to the last sixpence. Kelly would take 4d to give him a bed for the night at the lodging house and Eddowes would take the remaining 2d, which was just enough needed to stay at the Mile End Casual Ward.

During the afternoon of the 29th, Eddowes told Kelly that she was travelling to Bermondsey to visit her daughter, Catherine, who was married to a gun maker. Eddowes and Kelly separated at Houndsditch and she told Kelly that she expected to be back by 4 pm. Kelly then went to a pawn shop and pawned his boots and the money bought him a bed for the night at the lodging house, where he arrived at 8 pm, and where he remained throughout the night. Meanwhile, at 8.30 pm on the 29th, a group of people had gathered outside 29 Aldgate High Street. A passing policeman, PC Louis Frederick Robinson, saw the gathering, he walked over to them and quickly saw Eddowes was lying drunk on the pavement. Robinson then proceeded to get Eddowes on her feet and leaned her up against the shutters of the house, Eddowes then promptly slumped back down onto the pavement. Robinson called for assistance and PC George Simmons came to help. Eddowes was escorted to Bishopsgate Police Station, where she would be locked up until she was sober enough to be released. At the station she was asked her name, to which she replied 'Nothing' within half an hour she was fast asleep in her cell. At 12.30 am on the morning of the 30th, Eddowes awoke and asked PC George Hutt when they would be releasing her. Hutt replied to her 'when you are capable of taking care of yourself'. She was deemed capable of this at 1.00 am and upon her release, said to Hutt, 'All right. Good night, old cock.' Before leaving, she was asked once more by Hutt for her name, to which she replied, 'Mary Ann Kelly of 6 Fashion Street'. Eddowes walked out of the station and instead of turning right to take the shortest route to the lodging house at Flower and Dean Street, she turned left, which is the general direction of Aldgate. At 1.35 am she was observed by three people: Joseph Lawende, Joseph Hyam Levy, and Henry 'Harry' Harris, who had just left the Imperial Club in Duke's Place on Duke Street. Eddowes was seen by them – alive – in a narrow walkway called Church Passage. Lawende was to later describe Eddowes to be wearing a black jacket and bonnet whilst speaking with a man he described as of medium build with a fair moustache at the entrance to Church Passage. He said also she was facing the man, with one hand on his chest, but not in a way that suggested to him that she was resisting him. Lawende went on to say he believed the man with Eddowes to be 5 foot 7 inches tall and of about 30 years of age. He was also wearing a loose-fitting 'pepper and salt coloured loose jacket', a grey peaked cloth cap and a 'reddish' neckerchief. Lawende stated that he had walked past them both but did not look back as he did so. He also said the man gave the appearance of being a sailor. At 1.44 am, the mutilated and disembowelled body of Eddowes was discovered. Her head was turned to the left side and she was lying on her back in the south-west corner of Mitre Square. She was found by PC Edward Watkins who had only been in the vicinity just fourteen minutes earlier. Watkins immediately called for assistance from the night watchman at the Kearley and Tonge warehouse, who also happened to be an ex-policeman named George James Morris. Morris had been sweeping the landings as Watkins approached and said to him, 'For god's sake, mate, come to my assistance!' The pair went to the body of Eddowes and upon seeing it, Morris informed Watkins that he had heard nothing. This was also backed up by George Clapp, a night watchman at 5 Mitre Square. Richard Pearse, an off-duty policeman who resided at 3 Mitre Square also heard nothing. PC James Harvey was on his nightly beat within the area and he had walked down Church Passage from Duke Street at 1.30 am and was one of the first officers to arrive after hearing Morris' whistle for help. He also later said he'd not seen or heard anything. Local surgeon, George William Sequeira, was called for by another officer who attended the scene, PC Holland. Shortly before 2 am Sequeira arrived and was followed by police surgeon Frederick Gordon Brown minutes later. Next to follow were two pieces of evidence left near the crime scene. As of this point, nothing had ever been left behind by the Ripper. At around 2.55 am on the morning of the 30th, a blood-stained piece of Eddowes' apron was found at the bottom of a common stairway in Goulston Street, Whitechapel, by a PC Alfred Long. Long was adamant that the piece of apron had not been there when he passed the location at around 2.20 am. But perhaps of more significant importance was that above the apron, on a wall, was some graffiti written in chalk with letters some three-quarters of an inch in length that read, 'The Juwes are the men that will not be blamed for nothing'. The obvious implications of the message was to blame the Jewish population and it was often the case that graffiti of this nature was found around this particular area. A question asked at the time: was this the writing of the Ripper? Or was it simply by chance that the bloody apron was on the ground beneath it? The City of London police wanted to photograph the graffiti so that it could then be washed off for fear that the writing would incite potential racial unrest and riots. Charles Warren, the Metropolitan Police commissioner, ordered its removal at 5am before a picture could be taken. The post mortem of Eddowes was carried out by Frederick Gordon Brown and his findings were as follows:

> The body was on its back, the head turned to the left shoulder. The arms by the side of the body as if they had fallen there. Both palms upwards, the fingers slightly bent. A thimble was lying off the finger on the right side. The clothes drawn up above the abdomen. The thighs were naked. Left leg extended in a line

Catherine Eddowes

with the body. The abdomen was exposed. Right leg bent at the thigh and knee. The bonnet was at the back of the head - great disfigurement of the face. The throat was cut. Across below the throat was a neckerchief.... The intestines were drawn out to a large extent and placed over the right shoulder – they were smeared over with some feculent matter. A piece of about two feet was quite detached from the bod and placed between the body and the left arm, apparently by design. The lobe and auricle of the right ear were cut obliquely through. There was a quantity of clotted blood on the pavement on the left side of the neck round the shoulder and upper part of the arm, and fluid blood-coloured serum which had flowed under the neck to the right shoulder, the pavement sloping in that direction. Body was quite warm. No death suffering had taken place. She must have been dead most likely within the half hour. We looked for superficial bruises and saw none. No blood on the skin of the abdomen or secretion of any kind on the thighs. No spitting of blood on the bricks or pavement around. No marks of blood below the middle of the body. Several buttons were found in the clotted blood after the body was removed. There was no blood on the front of the clothes. There were no traces of recent connection.

Brown followed up in the afternoon with an examination of the body and stated:

After washing the left hand carefully, a bruise the size of a sixpence, recent and red, was discovered on the back of the left hand between the thumb and first finger. A few small bruises on the right shin of an older date. The hands and arms were bronzed. No bruises on the scalp, the back of the body, or the elbows. The face was very much mutilated. There was a cut about a quarter of an inch through the lower left eyelid, dividing the structure completely through. The upper eyelid on that side, there was a scratch through the skin on the left upper eyelid, near to the angle of the nose. The right eyelid was cut through to about half an inch. There was a deep cut over the bridge of the nose, extending from the left border of the nasal bone down near the angle of the jaw on the right side of the cheek. This cut went into the bone and divided all the structures of the cheek except the mucous membrane of the mouth. The tip of the nose was quite detached by an oblique cut from the bottom of the nasal bone to where the wings of the nose join on to the face. A cut from this divided the upper lip and extended through the substance of the gum over the right upper lateral incisor tooth… There was on each side of cheek a cut which peeled up the skin, forming a triangular flap about an inch and a half. On the left cheek there were two abrasions of the epithelium under the left ear…. The cause of death was haemorrhage from the left common carotid artery. The death was immediate and the mutilations were inflicted after death…. There would not be much blood on the murderer. The cut was made by someone on the right side of the body, kneeling below the middle of the body. The peritoneal lining was cut through on the left side and the left kidney carefully taken out and removed…. I believe the perpetrator of the act must have had considerable knowledge of the position of the organs in the abdominal cavity and the way of removing them. The parts removed would be of no use for any professional purpose. It required a great deal of knowledge to have removed the kidney and to know where it was placed. Such a knowledge might be possessed by one in the habit of cutting up animals. I think the perpetrator of this act had sufficient time…. It would take at least five minutes …. I believe it was the act of one person.

Again the suggestion of anatomical knowledge was made and even that was subject to debate. George Bagster Phillips agreed also that a certain level of knowledge must have been held by the Ripper, in that the mutilations incurred 'gave no evidence of anatomical knowledge in the sense that it evidenced the hand of a qualified surgeon'. It was his belief that the culprit may have only had the skill needed to be a butcher or general slaughterman. By stark contrast, police physician Thomas Bond said, 'in each case the mutilation was inflicted by a person who had no scientific nor anatomical knowledge. In my opinion he does not even possess the technical knowledge of a butcher or horse slaughterer or any person accustomed to cutting up dead animals'. This opinion was backed up by George Sequeira, who had been the first doctor to arrive to the murder scene of Eddowes, and William Sedgwick Saunders, the City of London medical officer, who had also been at the autopsy. Both men agreed that the attacker lacked anatomical knowledge and was not searching for any organs in particular.

The inquest opened on 4 October at the City of London Mortuary and was in the charge of Samuel F. Langham, the coroner for the city of London. Seven witnesses spoke on the first day. Eliza Gold, one of Eddowes' sisters, spoke to confirm that the deceased woman was indeed her sister and that she had last seen her some 'three to four weeks' earlier when Eddowes had visited her while sick. John Kelly spoke to identify Eddowes again, as well as to state that they had lived together for seven years and his last sighting of her had been at 2 pm on 29 September. He also testified that she typically earned money by selling goods though surprisingly said she seldom drank or lived by 'immoral purposes'. PC Edward Watkins testified to say that his beat was around twelve to fourteen minutes in length and when he'd passed through Mitre Square at 1.30 am, nothing had been out of place. He spoke of his actions upon arriving at the scene of the murder and made clear that he had not seen or heard anything at that time. In the first, architect Frederick Foster produced a plan of Mitre Square and explained how the murderer could walk from Berner Street (the site of the murder of Elizabeth Stride) to Mitre Street in just twelve minutes. Following directly from him was Inspector Collard of the City Police, who spoke of the scene of the crime and the actions of the police as well as assisting Drs Sequeira and Brown to the Golden

Lane Mortuary with the body of Eddowes. Dr Brown testified to state that Eddowes would have died quickly after the slashing of her throat and that she had died just thirty to forty minutes before his arrival. The wounds were, in his opinion, inflicted with a knife of around 6 inches in length after death with the attacker kneeling at her right side. Brown also again put forward his idea of the individual having knowledge of anatomy to remove the organs.

Proceedings were then adjourned until 11 October and on this date no fewer than fifteen witnesses were called. George Sequeira, spoke to confirm that he was the first medical person on scene and that he agreed with Dr Brown that the perpetrator was not one of great medical skill or anatomical knowledge. His testimony was followed by another medical officer by the name of William Saunders, who was to testify that no poisons were present in Eddowes' body. Catherine Phillips, the daughter of Eddowes, spoke of the troubled relationship she had with her parents and said that she'd not seen her father for over a year, and for two years in the case of her mother, and that she had even withheld her address from her mother as she would often be 'applying for money' from her. Next four police officers testified. The first three spoke of finding Eddowes drunk on Aldgate High Street, then of taking her to Bishopsgate Police Station, and then her release in the early hours of 30 September. George Morris spoke of being informed by PC Watkins of his discovery in Mitre Square and said, 'The constable said, "for god's sake, mate, come to my assistance" I said, "stop till I get my lamp. What is the matter?" "oh dear", he exclaimed, "here is another woman cut to pieces."' Morris made clear that he saw and heard nothing and that if the deceased had cried out during the attack, he would have heard it. PC James Harvey spoke to say that although his own beat took him just to Church Passage, he had also seen and heard nothing until Morris had blown his police whistle for assistance. Joseph Lawende testified to having 'observed a man and woman together at the corner of Church Passage.... Leading to Mitre Square' and approximately 'nine or ten feet' from him. He said that he had provided a description of the man to the police at the time but also he would not be able to recognise the man again. PC Alfred Long then testified to finding a 'portion of white apron', which was on the ground at the doorway to numbers 106–119 Goulston Street, and the graffiti written on the wall above which he'd written down the message in his pocketbook. He too had heard nor seen anything amiss at the time before he proceeded to go to the police station after telling another PC who had arrived on scene to 'keep observation on the dwelling house, and see if any one entered or left'. The concluding witness of the day and the proceedings was DC Daniel Halse, who testified he'd issued instructions 'for the neighbour to be searched and every man stopped and examined' after hearing of Eddowes' murder. He also said he'd been to Goulston Street to view the graffiti, where he had heard talk amongst the other officers that the word 'Juwes' should be erased from the wall and that the other writing remain, citing the reason of, 'the fear on the part of the Metropolitan Police (was) that the writing might cause riot was the side reason why (the graffito) was rubbed out'. Again following a brief deliberation, the jury, having been instructed to consider precisely how, when, and by what means Eddowes came about her death, returned a verdict of wilful murder against some person unknown. Each of the jurors also agreed to present their fees to Eddowes' daughter. The attack on Eddowes was the most southerly of the Ripper murders and, as such, fell within a different police jurisdiction; that of the City of London Police (compared to the Metropolitan Police for the other murders). Thus, DI James McWilliam of that force joined in the search for the killer, beginning with a house to house enquiry, but nothing was found.

Among Eddowes' possessions when she was found were a small mustard tin that contained two pawn tickets. One had been issued on 31 August in the name of Emily Birell, which was for the flannel shirt, the other to a Church Street pawnbroker named Smith, which was issued on 29 September to a Jane Kelly in relation to a pair of boots. This is indeed how John Kelly learned of her death as these details were published on 2 October with a description of the crudely drawn tattoo on her forearm. Eddowes was found to have no money upon her. The murderer most likely left the crime scene via St James's Place that led to Goulston Street (which is where the section of shawl was dropped).

On 1 October, a postcard was received by the Central News Agency and was later called the 'Saucy Jacky' postcard. It was written by the supposed killer and went into detail of the previous days' murders of Stride and Eddowes, which he described as the 'double event'. The authenticity of the postcard is still open to doubt today due to some believing that it was mailed before the murders took place but the card was actually postmarked more than a day after the killings took place, meaning that all the details within were widely reported prior to the author penning it. The postcard read as follows:

> I was not codding dear old Boss when I gave you the tip, you'll hear about saucy Jacky's work tomorrow double event this time number one squealed a bit couldn't finish straight off. Had not time to get ears off for police, thanks for keeping last letter back till I got to work again.
>
> Jack the Ripper

Police would later claim they had identified the author as a London-based journalist, which was readily dismissed. The Whitechapel murders were big business and the media were selling papers by the bucket load. Any lapse between murders would mean public interest would wane, so the ever-fertile imagination of the journalists would often be required to boost sales. Just over two weeks later on 16 October, a cubical parcel measuring 3.5 inches containing half a preserved human kidney was received by the chairman of the Whitechapel Vigilance Committee, George Lusk. It had with it the now notoriously known, 'From Hell' letter, and read as follows:

> From hell.
> Mr Lusk,
> Sor
> I send you half the Kidne I took from one women prasarved it for you tother piece I fried and ate it was very nise. I may

send you the bloody knif that took it out if you only wate a while longer

Signed
Catch me when you can Mishter Lusk

The letter was written in a style different from the 'Saucy Jacky' postcard and the spelling phrased to make the author of Irish descent, or at the very least, intending to make him appear to be Irish.

Lusk was persuaded to take the kidney to Dr Frederick Wiles who held a surgery at Mile End Road. Upon arriving it was found that Wiles was out and his assistant, F.S. Reed, examined the contents of the box before taking it to Dr Thomas Horrocks Openshaw at the nearby London Hospital. Openshaw examined it and believed it to be human, from the left side of the body, and preserved in spirits before being forwarded to Lusk. On 19 October, *The Daily Telegraph* reported that Openshaw had described the kidney as a 'ginny kidney' from a 45-year-old female. *The Star* reported the same day that Openshaw vehemently denied this, saying that neither the sex nor age could be determined, or even how long it was preserved in spirits. Being now in the public eye, Openshaw was to receive a letter of his own on 29 October, which reads:

> Old boss you was rite it was the left kidney i was goin to hoperate agin close to your ospitle just as i was going to dror mi nife along of er bloomin throte them cusses of coppers spoilt the game but i guess i wil be on the job soon and will send you another bit of innerds
>
> Jack the Ripper

O have you seen the delve with his mikerscope and scalpel a - lookin at a kidney with a slide cocked up.

Major Henry Smith, acting City of London Police commissioner, would later say in his memoirs, *From Constable to Commissioner* published in 1910, that the kidney Lusk received had been the one missing from Eddowes due to the length of the renal artery upon the kidney, which matched the missing length from the body, and that both her body and kidney received showed signs of Bright's disease (an inflammatory disease of the kidney known today as acute glomerulonephritis). Smith's recollection, like many of his tales, was subject to exaggeration (no doubt to boost sales) and the report on the kidney did not correspond to police nor pathologist reports of the time. Police surgeon Brown had even stated that the kidney had in fact been trimmed up and the renal artery was gone. Memos from the Metropolitan Police even stated that the kidney could have come from a body located within a hospital morgue. Saunders would later state that 'the right kidney of the woman Eddowes was perfectly normal in its structure and healthy post mortem... my opinion is that it was a student antic'. Chief Inspector Donald Swanson wrote later 'similar kidneys might and could be obtained from any dead person upon whom a post mortem had been made for any cause, by students or dissecting room porter'.

Catherine Eddowes was finally laid to rest on Monday, 8 October. Her grave was unmarked at 49336, square 318 in the City of London Cemetery. The service was conducted by the Reverend J. Dunscombe. The coffin was made of polished elm and the plate on it read simply;

Catherine Eddowes, died Sept.30, 1888, aged 43 years.

Dozens of people had lined the streets to pay their respects as the funeral cortege – which consisted of an open glass hearse – began its journey from Golden Lane Mortuary to the cemetery at precisely 1.30 pm. The mourning coach contained John Kelly, four of Eddowes' sisters, and two of her nieces. As the coffin arrived at the cemetery, a crowd of approximately 500 people were waiting outside.

CHAPTER 7

Mary Jane Kelly

Mary Jane Kelly was the last of 'The Canonical Five' victims of the Ripper (and even this is contested to being an actual Ripper murder). She was a women whom very little was known about, and what is known was gained from her own stories, which may very well have been fabricated due to a lack of evidence to back the claims up. According to Joseph Barnett, whom Kelly had lived with prior to her death, Kelly was born in 1863 in Limerick, Ireland and her family had relocated to Wales when she was a child. She had told Barnett that her family had been quite wealthy but had later disowned her, though she remained close to her sister. Her father, John Kelly, worked in an ironworks and she had seven brothers and at least one sister. One report on Kelly said she was 'an excellent scholar and an artist of no mean degree'. This was questioned later though when Barnett later said that she had asked him to read to her newspaper reports on the Ripper. In 1879, aged around 16, Kelly married a coal miner named Davis or Davies. The marriage lasted between two to three years, sadly because her husband was killed in a mining accident. She then moved in with a cousin who lived in Cardiff and it is believed that, aged around 20, she entered prostitution as a way to earn a living. She was described as being 5 feet 7 inches tall, 'quite attractive' and 'a pretty, buxom girl'. She apparently always wore a clean white apron but no hat. *The Daily Telegraph* called her, 'tall, slim, fair, of fresh complexion, and of attractive appearance'. In 1884 Kelly moved to London and found employment in Chelsea working for a tobacconist, before finding other employment as a domestic servant. A year later would find her living in the district of Fitzrovia in Central London. Shortly after this her luck improved when she found employment at a high-class brothel in the West End, where she was apparently one of the most popular girls there and would earn a decent wage, which she would spend on lavish clothes and travelling via carriage. Although life must have seemed good by 1885 she was living in the East End with a Mrs Buki near the London Docks North Quay. The reason for the fast move from West to East End is not known for certain but a guess could be a falling out with a pimp. Kelly then moved out of Buki's lodging house and took up lodgings with Mrs Carthy in Breezer's Hill, Ratcliffe Highway. She lived here for around a year until 1886 when she moved out and met a builder who Carthy believed Kelly married. Whether this is true or not is unclear but it is known that Kelly then moved further into the East End and took up residence with a man named Morgan Stone near the Commercial Gas Works in Stepney and then later with a Mason's plasterer named Joseph Flemming. We know that Kelly was living at a lodging house named Cooley's, located in Thrawl Street, Spitalfields, in 1886. Nothing further is known until 8 April when Kelly met Joseph Barnett, a 28-year-old who was employed as a fish porter at Billingsgate Market. Barnett took Kelly for a drink and the pair agreed to meet the following day. Things went very well on this second meeting as it resulted in the pair deciding to live together. They took residence at an address in George Street, near Commercial Street. From here they relocated to Little Paternoster Row, and this dwelling was to be home for only a short time due to them being evicted on the grounds of non-payment of rent and drunken disorderly behaviour. Next stop was a move to Brick Lane before finally relocating to Miller's Court off Dorset Street, around February and March of 1888. Number 13 Miller's Court is well known, of course, because it was photographed by the police while Kelly's body lay in situ after her death. Located at the back of 26 Dorset Street, Spitalfields, the room had, at one time, actually been the back parlour of the Dorset Street residence and had a wooden wall set up as a divide to create the 12 foot square room. The furnishing was sparse, having just a bed, three tables and a chair. A print of 'the fisherman's widow' hung above the fireplace. A small tin was placed beneath the bed. Natural lighting of the property was provided by two windows of irregular size that faced into the yard that contained a dustbin and tap that supplied them with water. The door of their premises opened onto a 26-foot-long arched passageway that connected with Miller's Court and Dorset Street. A gas lamp opposite this door illuminated it at night. One of the windows, the one closest to the door, was broken at the corner and Kelly, who had lost her key, would put her hand through the hole to bolt and unbolt the door from the outside. It was later claimed by a neighbour, Julia Venturney, that Kelly had broken the window and that it was often covered up inside with a man's coat to act as both a curtain and to block draughts from getting in. It had been noted by more than one person that Kelly wished for a return to her native Ireland and that the London lifestyle of depravity was making her miserable. Lizzie Albrook, a friend and neighbour of Kelly later recounted that Kelly was 'heartily sick' of her life's path by 1888 and wished to return to Ireland 'where her people lived'. Kelly's landlord, John McCarthy, also said 'she was a very quiet woman when sober but noisy when in drink'. One of Kelly's nicknames was 'Dark Mary', this name was obtained by her reputation of becoming abusive and temperamental when under the influence of alcohol. Misfortune fell upon Barnett in July 1888 as he lost his job as a fish porter due to stealing. This led Kelly back into ways of prostitution and Barnett would later say she would allow other prostitutes to sleep in their room on 'cold, bitter nights', due to Kelly not having the heart to turn them away. Barnett initially agreed to this until one night Barnett and Kelly argued over a prostitute known only to him as 'Julia'. This would lead to Barnett leaving Miller's Court on 30 October and moving to 24–25 New Street, Bishopsgate. Though he had moved out, he still would visit Kelly on a daily basis during 1–8 November and would, on occasion, give her money. The day before her murder, Barnett paid a visit to Kelly between the hours of 7 and 8 pm. Kelly was entertaining a friend of hers called Maria Harvey. Barnett soon made his excuses and left, only to apologise for not having any money to give her. He returned to his lodging house and proceeded to play cards with the other residents until he fell asleep at 12.30 am. Kelly's friend, Lizzie Albrook, had also paid a visit to Kelly, who was sober and said to her, 'Whatever you do, don't you do wrong and turn out as I have'. It is known that earlier that evening Kelly had frequented and had one drink at the Ten Bells pub with a woman named Elizabeth Foster. Kelly was then seen with two friends drinking later that evening at the Horn of Plenty pub located on Dorset Street. Kelly was late seen drunk and in the company of a stout, ginger-haired man aged around 36 at 11.45 pm by a fellow resident of Miller's Court, Mary Ann Cox, a 31-year-old prostitute. She also described the man as wearing a black felt bowler hat, having a thick moustache, blotches on his face and carrying a can of beer. At this point Cox and Kelly bid each other goodnight before Kelly cheerfully said to Cox, 'I am going to have a song'. With this Kelly took the man into her lodgings while Cox returned to her own dwelling at number 5 Miller's Court. Cox then heard Kelly sing aloud the song, 'A Violet from Mother's Grave'. When Cox left her dwelling at midnight, Kelly was heard to be singing still, and was still singing Cox returned at 1 am. At 1.30 am Kelly had fallen silent as stated later by Elizabeth Prater, who lived directly above Kelly. At this point, unemployed labourer George Hutchinson, who was acquainted with Kelly, said he met her at 2 am on Flower and Dean Street and said Kelly had asked to borrow sixpence. Hutchinson claimed that he was broke due to visiting Romford the previous day. He said that Kelly then walked off in the direction of Thrawl Street and that a man approached her of 'Jewish appearance' and aged around 34 or 35. Hutchinson then hung around because although Kelly seemed to be friends with him he found him to be suspicious. According to Hutchinson the man had also attempted to hide his features, by lowering down his head with his hat over his eyes as Kelly and the man passed him. Incredibly, Hutchinson was able to provide the police with an amazing description of the man given the lighting conditions available at that time even noting the colour of the eyelashes. Hutchinson also claimed to hear them talking in the street opposite the court where Kelly was living, Kelly had apparently complained of losing her handkerchief, and the man offered her one of his own. Hutchinson then apparently heard Kelly say, 'Alright my dear, come along. You will be comfortable.' They then both walked into 13 Miller's Court and Hutchinson followed. He saw neither of them again and left at 2.45 am. Mary Ann Cox left her residence at 1 am to return at 3 am and reported hearing no sound or seeing any light coming from Kelly's room but did later say she thought someone left there at around 5.45 am. Between 3.30 am and 4 am, Elizabeth Prater, who lived above Kelly, said she had been awoken by her kitten walking over her neck. Sarah Lewis, who had slept that night at number 2 Miller's Court, both said they heard a faint cry of 'Murder!' but neither paid any attention to it as it was common to hear such cries in this part of London. Lewis went on to say it was 'Only one scream. I took no notice of it.' She also said that she did not sleep that night and that she heard people moving around the court during the early hours. Prater also reported leaving her abode at 5.30 am to go to the Ten Bells pub for a drink of rum but said she saw nothing out of the ordinary. Friday, 9 November was the day of the annual Lord Mayor's Day. This was the day that Kelly's landlord, John McCarthy, decided that the rents owing to him by her – some six weeks' worth, totalling 29 shillings in value – would be collected. He sent his assistant, Thomas Bowyer, an ex-soldier, to collect it on his behalf. At approximately 10.45 am, Bowyer knocked on Kelly's door but received no response. He tried turning the handle but discovered the door was locked. He then looked through the keyhole but saw nobody inside, so pushed the clothing that was used to block the windowpane aside, along with the muslin curtains, and then saw the horrific sight of Kelly's mutilated body lying on the bed. It was believed that she had been murdered some three to nine hours prior to discovery. No doubt in terror and shock, Bowyer ran to report his find to his boss, McCarthy, who went with Bowyer to verify his claims before telling Bowyer to inform Commercial Street Police Station. Upon arrival at the station, Bowyer stammered out to the officer, 'Another one, Jack the Ripper. Awful, [John] McCarthy sent me.' The inspector, Walter Beck, then went with Bowyer to Miller's Court, and immediately requested assistance from police surgeon George Bagster Phillips. Beck also gave orders preventing anyone from entering or exiting the yard. Beck arranged for news of this latest Ripper murder to be telegraphed to Scotland Yard, and requested the assistance of bloodhounds. Also to attend was Superintendent Thomas Arnold and Inspector Edmund Reid from Whitechapel's H Division, as well as Frederick Abberline and Robert Anderson, from Scotland Yard, who arrived at the scene between 11.30 am and 1 pm. The news of the latest murder spread fast and before long a crowd of over 1,000 people had gathered at each end of Dorset Street. After a month of no murders the public no doubt were anxious that it had started up again and they voiced their frustrations at the police. The bloodhounds idea was decided to be futile, and with that the order was delivered from Arnold to break into the room at 1.30 pm. It was discovered that the fire in the room had burned so fiercely that even the solder between the kettle and spout had melted into the grate of the fire, and that the ferocity of the fire had been caused by Kelly's clothes being thrown onto it. Inspector Abberline opined that this had been done by the murderer in an attempt to gain maximum light for him to be able to see during the attack. The room was otherwise lit by just a single candle that Kelly had purchased two days prior on 7 November. Two official crime scene photographs were taken before Kelly's body was taken from Miller's Court to the mortuary in Shoreditch, where her body was formerly identified by Joseph Barnett, who was only able to recognise Kelly's body by 'the ear and the eyes'. John McCarthy also viewed the body at the mortuary and was likewise certain the body was that of Kelly. The post mortem of Kelly's body was extensive and took two-and-a-half hours to perform. The injuries that she had been subjected to had been by far the worst seen on any victim yet, no doubt due to the murder being committed in a room, the murderer afforded the time to perform his every desire. The body was examined by Thomas Bond and George Bagster Phillips. They both concluded that death was around twelve hours before examination and Phillips opined that the mutilations would have taken two hours to perform, whilst Bond noted that rigor mortis set in as the body was being examined, and this would indicate death had occurred between 2 and 8 am. Bond's full document of the circumstances read as follows:

The body was lying naked in the middle of the bed, the head was turned on the left cheek, the left arm was close to the body with the forearm flexed at a right angle and lying across the abdomen. The right arm was slightly abducted from the body and rested on the mattress. The elbow was bent, the forearm supine with the fingers clenched. The legs were wide apart, the left thigh at right angles to the trunk and the right forming an obtuse angle with the pubis. The whole of the surface of the abdomen and thighs was removed and the abdominal cavity emptied of its viscera. The breasts were cut off, the arms mutilated by several jagged wounds and the face hacked beyond recognition of the features. The tissues of the neck were severed all round down to the bone. The viscera were found in various parts viz: the uterus and kidneys with one breast under the head, the other breast by the right foot, the liver between the feet, the intestines by the right side and the spleen by the left side of the body. The flaps removed from the abdomen and thighs were on a table. The bed clothing at the right corner was saturated with blood, and on the floor beneath was a pool of blood covering about two feet square. The wall by the right side of the bed and in a line with the neck was marked by blood which had struck it in several places. The face was gashed in all directions, the nose, cheeks, eyebrows, and ears being partly removed. The lips were blanched and cut by several incisions running obliquely down to the chin. There were also numerous cuts extending irregularly across all the features. The neck was cut through the skin and other tissues right down to the vertebrae, the fifth and sixth being deeply notched. The skin cuts in the front of the neck showed distinct ecchymosis. The air passage was cut at the lower part of the larynx through the cricoid cartilage. Both breasts were more or less removed by circular incisions, the muscle down to the ribs being attached to the breasts. The intercostals between the forth, fifth, and sixth ribs were cut through and the contents of the thorax visible through the openings. The skin and tissues of the abdomen from the costal arch to the pubes were removed in three large flaps. The right thigh was denuded in front of the bone, the flap of skin, including the external organs of generation, and part of the right buttock. The left thigh was stripped of skin fascia, and muscles as far as the knee. The left calf showed a long gash through skin and tissues to the deep muscles and reached from the knee to five inches above the ankle. Both arms and forearms had extensive jagged wounds. The right thumb showed a small superficial incision about one inch long, with extravasation of blood in the skin, and there were several abrasions on the back of the hand moving over showing the same condition. On opening the thorax it was found that the right lung was minimally adherent by old firm adhesions. The lower part of the lung was broken and torn away. The left lung was intact. It was adherent at the apex and there were a few adhesions over the side. In the substances of the lung, there were several nodules of consolidation. The pericardium was open below and the heart absent. In the abdominal cavity, there was some partly digested food of fish and potatoes, and similar food was found in the remains of the stomach attached to the intestines.

Phillips was of the opinion that Kelly had been killed by a slash to the throat and the mutilations performed afterwards. Bond believed the knife used was about 1 inch wide and at the very least 6 inches in length and was of the opinion that the murderer did not have any medical knowledge. He wrote:

> In each case the mutilation was inflicted by a person who had no scientific nor anatomical knowledge. In my opinion, he does not even possess the technical knowledge of a butcher or horse slaughterer or a person accustomed to cutting up dead animals.

Shoreditch Town Hall was the scene of the inquest which began on Monday, 12 November. Presiding over the inquest was the coroner for North East Middlesex, Roderick Macdonald MP. Upon being sworn in, the jury were taken by Inspector Abberline to view Kelly's body in the mortuary adjoining Shoreditch Church and then on to the scene of the murder in Miller's Court. This took approximately an hour before the jurors returned to Shoreditch Town Hall to hear the witness testimonies.

Joseph Barnett testified first and said he had lived with Kelly for 'one year and eight months' before the pair had separated following an argument on 30 October about Kelly allowing 'a woman of bad character' to stay in her room, whom she'd 'taken in out of compassion'. He maintained that he'd stayed on good terms with Kelly after the separation and that he'd seen her alive at approximately 7.45 pm on 8 November. On the final occasion he had seen Kelly, she had been 'quite sober'. When talking of her background, Barnett told of her marriage at age 16, her relocation to Cardiff upon the death of her husband and of her Irish origins. Barnett also pushed the idea that her cousin was, in his opinion, the person who'd introduced Kelly into prostitution: 'she was following a bad life with her cousin, who, as I reckon and as I often told her, was the cause of her downfall'. Following on from Barnett, Thomas Bowyer told how he'd discovered the body on 9 November. He spoke of first observing two pieces of flesh on the bedside table, then seeing Kelly's extensively mutilated body. He 'at once went very quickly' to John McCarthy to inform him of his find. McCarthy had himself looked through the window to confirm the sight that had befallen Bowyer, before they went off to the nearest police station. McCarthy then said that Bowyer had informed him, 'Guv'nor, I knocked at the door, and could not make anyone answer. I looked through the window and saw a lot of blood'. They had both then reported their discovery to Inspector Reid at Commercial Street Police Station. McCarthy also stated that Kelly's rent was in arrears by 29 shillings. In regard to her character, McCarthy described Kelly as an 'exceptionally quiet woman'. When sober, but that 'when in drink she had a lot more to say'. Mary Ann Cox also spoke stating that she had known Kelly for eight months and that her last sighting of Kelly had been in Dorset Street at 11.45 pm on 8 November where Kelly was 'very much intoxicated' Cox described the short, stout and shabbily dressed man in her company, who had been holding a pot of ale in his hand. Cox also said she'd not heard any sound from Kelly's room and upon returning to her own apartment at 5 Miller's Court at 3 am it was still silent. Elizabeth Prater stated she'd heard a 'suppressed cry' of 'Oh! Murder!' at around 3.45 am. She claimed that such cries were however commonplace in and around Spitalfields. Also to testify were Caroline Maxwell and Sarah Lewis. Maxwell said she'd seen Kelly alive on the morning of 9 November Lewis said she'd seen a stout man in a black wide awake hat standing in the courtyard in the early hours and hearing a woman cry 'Murder!' at 'nearly four'. Phillips then testified as to his examination of the body at 13 Miller's Court. He stated he'd arrived at the scene at 11.45 am and examined the body at 1.30 pm. He saw Kelly lying 'two-thirds over, towards the edge of the bedstead'. He was also certain the murderer had moved her body to perform the eviscerations. He opined the attack had taken place as Kelly had lain on the right side of the bed, and the cause of her death was the severance of her right carotid artery. A large quantity of blood under the bedstead, and the palliasse, pillow and sheet at the top of the bed were saturated with blood. The blood splattering on the wall on the right side of the bed in line with Kelly's neck also pointed to this opinion being correct. He deduced the time of death as being between 2 am and 8 am and that her last meal of fish and potatoes, which had moved into her intestines, had indicated it was consumed some time between 10 and 11 pm on 8 November. The blade was at least 6 inches long and 1 inch thick. The superficial wound to her thumb was also no doubt a defensive wound. More eyewitness and character testimonies followed. Julia Venturney and Maria Harvey spoke, before inspectors Beck and Abberline testified to their examination and response to the crime scene, including how Beck gave orders to the police surgeon at the scene, what he did to recover evidence and his orders that forbade the public from entering Miller's Court, and also the residents of the court not being allowed to leave their dwellings until everyone had been fully questioned by the police. Abberline spoke to state that Superintendent Arnold had ordered the door to Kelly's room be forced open with the aid of a pickaxe at 1.30 pm. He also testified about the findings within the room adding his belief that the amount of clothing in the fireplace had been put there by the murderer so that the resultant light from the burning garments gave him the light needed to perform his atrocity, the only light available before was a candle atop a piece of broken wine glass.

Abberline was the last to testify of the twelve witnesses, and everything was completed in a single day. Macdonald told the jury that they should adjourn to hear further testimony at a later date or close the procedures. He said, 'My own opinion is that it is very unnecessary for two courts to deal with these cases, and go through the same evidence, time after time, which only causes expense and trouble. If the coroner's jury can come to a decision as to the cause of death, then that is all that they have to do.... From what I learn, the police are content to take the future conduct of the case. It is for you to say whether you will close the inquiry today: if not, we shall adjourn for a week or fortnight, to hear the evidence that you may desire.'

After a short deliberation the jury returned a unanimous verdict: 'Wilful murder against some person or persons unknown'.

Bond wrote a report on 10 November that officially linked the murders of Mary Ann Nichols, Annie Chapman, Elizabeth Stride and Catherine Eddowes. His was also the first known offender profile that stated that the person responsible for these atrocities was a solitary eccentric who underwent bouts of periodic homicidal and erotic mania, and who had been in an extreme state of satyriasis as he performed the attacks on the five women. With this murder having taken place everything went quiet in Whitechapel, much to the relief of both the public and police. The police would now start to step down their enquiries. The murder and especially the mutilations performed upon Mary Jane Kelly were by far the worst committed upon any of the Ripper victims and even today some conjecture is raised as to whether she was an actual victim of him or if it was a copy-cat killing.

CHAPTER 8

The Suspects

It has been almost 140 years since Jack the Ripper carried out his brutal autumn of terror killings. In the following years since then dozens of names have been put forward as being responsible. Some hold strong claims and some are frankly ludicrous and it seems that at one time, any person of social standing in 1888 was named as the killer. As we stand today, there are seventeen names that are either of great interest or warrant further investigation and they are as follows:

Montague John Driutt
Aaron Kosmiński
Walter Sickert
Dr Francis Tumblety
James Maybrick
Joseph Barnett
Seweryn Antonowicz
  Kłosowski/George Chapman
Michael Ostrog

Dr Thomas Neill Cream
Prince Albert Victor
William Henry Bury
Nathan Kaminsky/David Cohen
Thomas Hayne Cutbush
James Kelly
Sir John Williams
George Hutchinson
Charles Allen Lechmere/Cross

Montague John Druitt

Druitt was born on 15 August 1857 in Wimborne Minster, Dorset. His family were upper-middle class. His father, William, was a surgeon. Druitt was educated at Winchester College and showed great sporting abilities, especially in cricket and fives (hand-tennis). His academic career was virtually impeccable and in 1876 he was awarded a Winchester Scholarship to New College, Oxford. At New College, Druitt was elected steward of the junior common room. He played cricket and rugby for the college team, and was a winner of both double and single fives at the university in 1877. Druitt attained a second class in Classical Moderations in 1878 and graduated with a third class Bachelor of Arts degree in *Literae Humaniores* (classics) in 1880. His intention was always to become a barrister. In 1882 Druitt was admitted to the Inner Temple, one of the qualifying bodies for English barristers. He was called to the Bar on 29 April 1885 and set up a practice as a barrister and special pleader. Later that year in September, Druitt's father died suddenly of a heart attack and left an estate worth £16,579 (£1,905,000 today). Druitt was to receive very little of this money due to him borrowing nearly £500 (£54,000 today) in 1882, which his father had told him was his legacy upon his death to pay for his membership fees to the Inner Temple. He did, however, receive his father's personal effects. Druitt rented chambers at 9 King's Bench Walk in the Inner Temple. Although one would think that being a barrister would be a prosperous living, it must be remembered that only the rich in the Victorian era could afford legal services. Some claim that he succeeded as a barrister and made a good income, whilst others claim Druitt hardly made enough to survive, struggling to pay the lease of the chambers. In 1886 he was listed as active in the Western Circuit and Winchester sessions and in 1887, active in the Western Circuit and Hampshire, Portsmouth, and Southampton Assizes. Whether he was successful or not is not conclusively known, but what is known is that to supplement his legal training, Druitt worked as an assistant schoolmaster at George Valentine's boarding school, 9 Eliot Place, Blackheath, London from 1888. The post came with lodgings at the distinguished school. His life should really have been a good one as he was fortunate enough to have a good start and high prospects, but on Friday, 30 November 1888, Druitt was dismissed from his post at the Blackheath boys' school. Again, with much of his life, the reason for this is unclear. *Acton, Chiswick & Turnham Green Gazette*, published on 5 January 1889, would later write that Druitt's brother, William, said at the inquest that his brother 'had got into serious trouble' but didn't specify any more detail. In early December 1888 he disappeared, and it was noted on 21 December that he was removed as treasurer and secretary from the Blackheath Cricket Club as they were of the belief that he had gone abroad. On New Year's Eve 1888 the body of Druitt was found floating in the River Thames off Thornycroft torpedo works, Chiswick, by a waterman named Henry Winslade. It was discovered that Druitt had stones in his pockets, which had kept his body submerged for a month. Upon him was a return train ticket to Hammersmith which was dated 1 December, a silver watch, a cheque for £50, and £16 in gold which, respectively, are worth £5,900 and £1,900 today. To be carrying the modern day equivalent of almost £8,000 is very strange and the source of this money is still unknown but an educated guess would perhaps suggest that this may have been his final pay from the school. His dismissal has long been a matter of conjecture, though the leading belief is that Druitt was homosexual or even pederast (a man who has a sexual relationship with a boy) and upon him being found out and consequently dismissed, he had been driven to commit suicide. Some speculate that the money on him was perhaps intended for a blackmailer. Another train of thought is that Druitt was not homosexual but was actually suffering from mental health issues, something that ran in the family. It is known that his mother suffered from depression and was placed in an institution in July 1888, where she was to stay until her death in 1890. His maternal grandmother committed suicide while classed insane, his aunt attempted suicide, and his eldest sister committed suicide in old age. In Druitt's room in Blackheath a note was found addressed to his brother William that read: 'Since Friday I felt that I was going to be like mother, and the best thing for me was to die'.

An inquest was held on 2 January 1889 at the Lamb Tap pub, Chiswick, by Dr Thomas Bramah Diplock. The jury concluded that Druitt had committed suicide by drowning while in an unsound state of mind. Druitt was laid to rest in Wimborne Cemetery on 3 January 1889. His estate was determined at £2,600 (equivalent to £308,100 today).

The Ripper Connection

This is most likely an association that was started by Henry Richard Farquharson, MP for West Dorset, in February 1891, when he stated that Jack the Ripper was, 'the son of a surgeon' and had committed suicide on the night of the final murder. Farquharson didn't venture as to name his suspect but given the description, it is rather coincidental that he knew the Druitt family (he lived just 10 miles from them) and moved within the same social circles when Druitt's father was a surgeon. Could Druitt have realistically been the killer? It is certainly true that after his suicide the murders stopped. Assistant Chief Constable Sir Melville Macnaghten was to name Druitt in a private handwritten memorandum that was dated 23 February 1894. He noted particularly Druitt's disappearance and death shortly after the last of the five murders. He also alluded that 'From private information I have little doubt that his own family suspected this man of being the Whitechapel Murderer; it was alleged that he was sexually insane.' He continued, 'I have always held strong opinions regarding him, and the more I think the matter over, the stronger these opinions become. The truth, however, will never be known, and did indeed at one time lie at the bottom of the Thames, if my conjunctions be correct!'

The validity of Macnaghten's claim must be put into question, however, because the notes within Scotland Yard files state that Druitt was a 41-year-old doctor rather than a 31-year-old solicitor. One can see that the murderer's MO would strongly favour a doctor but was Macnaghten misinformed about the profession of Druitt? Even with this all said, there is next to no evidence that Druitt was the murderer. There is the obvious conclusion to be made with his mental state but other than that there is very little to go on. Druitt didn't have an arrest file nor was he even spoken of in a way that made him out to be of an aggressive nature. Witness testimony must also be mentioned. The age estimate of 31 was close to Druitt's age. Three witnesses said the murderer had a moustache, Druitt did not. The description was also a man of medium to heavy build and also stout and broad shouldered. By contrast Druitt was a slender build man. Yet another problem with Druitt being a serious candidate for being the Ripper is that there was no night-train rail service between London and Blackheath, where he lived at the time of the murders. The last train would leave just past midnight and the first daily train leaving just past 5 am, which would cause a problem with any quick escape from a murder scene. He had law chambers at 9 King's Bench Walk, which was within walking distance of the crimes, but even taking this into account, it still makes Druitt an unlikely suspect. It has to be remembered that Druitt's passion was for cricket, and a glance at the declared players for matches around the time show him to have been playing on days of the murders. On 1 September, the day following the Nichols murder, he participated for Canford, Dorset, against Wimborne at Canford. On 8 September, the day following the Chapman murder, he was at the Rectory Field, Blackheath, for the 11.30 am start of a match against Christopherson brothers. One has to remember that Chapman was killed at around 5.30 am so would he have had time to kill her, change his bloodstained clothes, rest, have breakfast and then turn out for the starting X1 at 11.30 am? And he was in top form for the match, taking three wickets. This would be quite some ask of a man patrolling the streets of London the previous night on the look-out for a victim to kill. Of course, it certainly isn't impossible for a person not to perform these tasks, but I feel given these circumstances and considering his character, Druitt should be removed from the suspect list.

Aaron Kosmiński

Another name that has a long association with the Ripper is Aaron Kosmiński, or to give him his birth name, Aron Mordke Kozmiński, who was born on 11 September 1865 in Kłodawa, Poland. He emigrated from Poland in 1880 or 1881 and spent some time living with his sisters' families in Germany. The family then moved to London between 1881 and 1882. In London, Kosmiński took up a trade as a barber in Whitechapel. It has to be said at this point that Kosmiński didn't work all the time as a barber and that his work ethic was somewhat hit and miss. He may therefore have relied on financial support from his family as well as living with them, going

The Suspects

back and forth from addresses at 3 Sion Square and 16 Greenfield Street between the years 1890 and 1891 respectively. It was on 12 July 1890 that Kosmiński ended up in Mile End Old Town Workhouse because of his mental health. He was released three days later and eventually would end up back there on 4 February 1891. This time he was transferred to the Colney Hatch Lunatic Asylum. He remained there for 3 years until he was taken to Leavesden Asylum on 19 April 1894. His notes stated that by this time he had been suffering from mental illness for at least 9 years and that his 'madness' was in the form of auditory hallucinations, a paranoid fear of being fed by other people that led him to eat food from the gutter, and his refusal to wash or bathe. The Victorian explanation for this mania was given as 'self-abuse', which, when translated to modern-day language, means masturbation. His poor diet meant he was underweight, being recorded as just 44kg (6 stone, 9 pounds) in February 1919. Aaron Kosmiński passed away a month later aged just 53 years old.

The Ripper Connection
Kosmiński was directly mentioned as a suspect by Sir Melville Macnaghten, assistant chief constable of the London Metropolitan Police, in an 1894 memorandum where he named the Ripper as a Polish Jew called 'Kosmiński'. His reasoning for this was because Kosmiński apparently 'had a great hatred of women' and 'strong homicidal tendencies'. It is of note that Kosmiński, during his time in the asylum, was not known to show any aggression outside of brandishing a chair on one occasion and was only taken into custody because he drew a knife on one of his sisters. These two acts of violence are the only ones documented and within the asylum he was known to be quiet. It is also noteworthy that in the asylum he spoke only in his native language, Yiddish. This is a strong indication that he either wasn't comfortable speaking English or couldn't speak much of the language at all. This would mean it was unlikely he would have any confidence when approaching prostitutes. It must also be noted that at the time of the murders he was 23 years old and rather slim, due to his eating habits, and people had said the Ripper was

around 35–40 and of a well built nature. So, one has to ask how he ever became a suspect in the first place. Contrary to popular belief, Kosmiński was never officially named by the police force investigating the Ripper but Chief Inspector Swanson believed Kosmiński was to be placed high on the list of suspects. Memoirs from Sir Robert Anderson in 1910 also mentioned Kosmiński and his violent outbursts with a knife that led to his arrest. This now becomes rather dubious due to Anderson stating that Kosmiński had died a short time after his arrest, but Kosmiński was to live until 1919. Anderson also made the claim that Kosmiński was actually identified to be Jack the Ripper but the witness was not prepared to testify against a fellow Jew. This was never proven. So just how likely was Kosmiński of being the Ripper? The answer is it is highly unlikely he was. He was clearly a man who was in need of help given his mental illness but there is no indication that he was a psychopathic killer – he wasn't prone to continual violent outbursts and it appears that he didn't have the mental capacity to plan such attacks. He didn't have anatomical knowledge, he wasn't comfortable speaking English and certainly didn't fit the age or physical description given by eyewitnesses. My belief is that Aaron Kosmiński was an unfortunate person because of his illness and was made an easy target due to him being a Jew and I truly believe his name should be removed from the history books as having any association with the case and that he should be allowed to rest in peace.

Walter Sickert

Sickert has been linked to the case by several people over the years and probably most notably by the author Patricia Cornwell who named him as the murderer in her 2002 book, *Portrait of A Killer: Jack the Ripper – Case Closed*. Cornwell was fortunate because she was in a position to utilise the very latest techniques of forensics at that time to prove that Sickert was the elusive murderer, and upon the release of her book and the subsequent tour to promote it, she even told a US chat show, 'I do believe 100 per cent that Walter Richard Sickert committed those serial crimes'. Walter Richard Sickert was born on 31 May 1860 in Munich, Germany. His mother, Eleanor, was

English, his father, Oswald, was Danish. Oswald was an artist in Germany and was an illustrator for a comic journal. In 1868 the family decided to move to Bradford, England, before then moving to London in 1869. In 1878, aged 18, Sickert left school but was unable to pay for university, and though he had a shared love of his father's passion for art, he was dissuaded to follow a career in it by his father. The young Sickert decided to turn his hand to the stage, where he gained some small success, but it was a meeting with American artist, James McNeill Whistler, in May 1879 that would change his life. Sickert eventually turned painter and exhibited his works at the Fine Art Society in London in 1881. In October of that year he signed up for classes at both the Slade School of Fine Art and the Heatherley School of Art in London, which he dropped out of in 1882 when Whistler invited him to become his pupil and studio assistant. In 1885, he married Ellen Cobden, daughter of Liberal politician, Richard Cobden, who was twelve years his senior. They would eventually take a marital home at 54 Broadhurst Gardens, South Hampstead, where Sickert would use the top floor as a studio.

The Ripper Connection
It is claimed that Sickert was impotent, something caused by a series of operations as a child for a fistula of the penis. This had left him mentally scarred and with a deep hatred of women, which in turn would result in him committing the Ripper murders. There is a flaw in this theory instantly because St Mark's Hospital where the operations were performed specialised in rectal fistulas as opposed to genital ones. Just how truthful was it that Sickert was impotent? Here we must note that he divorced his wife in 1899, with his wife citing his constant infidelities and 'chronic independence' as reasons for the separation. It is also claimed that he was father to at least one illegitimate child. With this we can clearly say that impotence was not a factor. We must now try to find the hatred for women in his character. There is none that stands out other than his paintings, especially one that depicted the murder of a prostitute in Camden Town in 1908 named Emily Dimmock. His works did portray scenes of murder and he did have a fascination of this type of crime but that alone is hardly enough to label him the Ripper. But before we can completely

Sickert of all involvement we must know of his movements at the time. To be able to prove he was at the scenes of the crime is imperative, or at least in the vicinity of them, but there's strong evidence that Sickert was not even in the country at the time of the murders. A number of letters from his family referred to him being on holiday in France (a country he himself called his 'spiritual home') during most of the murders. Some people tried to get around this by saying that Sickert would pop over the Channel to commit a murder before then popping back to France to resume his holiday. This of course is quite a far-fetched idea, because if he wanted to commit murder, surely he would have done so in France, rather than extensively travel to do so? It is of note that Cornwell had several envelopes and stamps DNA tested in the belief that Sickert had written the Ripper letters, the theory being of course that the saliva he used to stick down the envelopes or attach the stamps would prove he was the author of letters. The common consensus today is the letters definitely show that numerous people penned the letters. That said, one letter did indicate a match – the Dr Openshaw letter. Many critics of the DNA resting state that it was based upon mitochondrial DNA and this can be shared between 1 and 10 per cent of the population, making the match to Sickert inconclusive. Another possible link was that the Dr Openshaw letter, as well as the two other Ripper letters and no less than eight letters written by Sickert that are to hand as evidence were all written on paper with a watermark of the Aberdeen paper maker Alexander Pirie and Sons. But this paper was widely in use from 1885 and 1887 and so all that can be deduced from this is that Sickert could have written some of the hoax letters, which is of course not proof that he had anything to do with the actual murders. Sickert was to marry again in 1911 to a student of his, Christine Angus, who was seventeen years his junior. Christine sadly passed away in 1920, aged just 53. It was alleged that Sickert exhibited bizarre behaviour at her graveside, where he supposedly opened the urn containing her ashes and proceeded to throw some of those ashes at the gathered mourners. This behaviour was a sign of a breakdown and grief, and after this he became more erratic and eccentric. In February of 1922 his mother passed away, which would only add to his depression. His life appeared to pick up when, in 1926, he married once more, but sadly this happiness was short lived because he suffered a possible stroke just a month after his marriage in July of that year. He took a year to recover and whilst he would continue with his work, he would only paint from photographs he acquired. In 1941, he was given a one-man exhibition at the National Gallery in London. The following year he died aged 81 in Bath, England, the city he'd spent his final years in. Walter Sickert undoubtedly had a morbid obsession with the Ripper case but cannot be considered a potential suspect for the killer due to the fact that he was outside of the country for a great deal of 1888.

Dr Francis Tumblety

Francis Tumblty, born in 1833, was an Irish-born American quack doctor who toured North America and amassed a small fortune with his fake medicines and elixirs. He was an eccentric person who would often visit Europe and even made wild claims such as he met with King William of Germany, Charles Dickens and even Louis Napoléon, president of France.

He was a resident of Whitechapel at the time of some of the murders and the Metropolitan police arrested him on 7 November 1888 on unrelated charges of gross indecency, which was most likely a homosexual act that at the time was illegal for which his bail was set at a hefty £300 (£42,000 in today's money). While out on bail he fled to France on the 20 November before quickly returning to America on the 24th of that month.

The Ripper Connection

It was Chief Inspector John Littlechild who, in 1913, first mentioned the name Tumblety to journalist George Sims as a suspect for being the Ripper. Littlechild had been head of the Metropolitan Police's Special Irish Branch during and after the time of the Whitechapel murders, (he'd actually been in office 1883–1893). Littlechild had (as far as known) very little to do with the murder investigations because he would have been occupied within his own role, but as a senior officer in the force he would have no doubt been able to communicate with Sir Robert Anderson and Chief Inspector Swanson. George Sims had written to Littlechild to ask if he had knowledge of a Dr D. who was rumoured to be connected to the murders. Sims had obviously been referring to Montague John Druitt, whose name had been linked to the case for at least 15 years by the time 1913 had arrived. Littlechild duly wrote back though to proclaim that he'd never heard of a Dr D. ever being associated with the case but did state the following, 'amongst the suspects, and to my mind a very likely one, was a Dr T. (who) was an American quack named Tumblety'.

He would continue to say that Tumblety had even been arrested for 'unnatural offences', that he had been remanded on bail, which he then jumped, making haste for Boulogne, and after this he was never heard from again. Littlechild would conclude, 'It was believed he committed suicide but certain it is that from that time the "Ripper" murders came to an end'. Indeed, Dr Tumblety had been arrested for and charged regarding acts of gross indecency with a number of men on 7 November 1888. Tumblety had also jumped bail and fled for Boulogne as Littlechild had stated. But one thing he was wrong on was the suicide because Tumblety had travelled home to America after fleeing to Boulogne. He arrived in New York but quickly had both the press and police on his trail and Inspector Byrnes of the New York police put him under surveillance. When questioned by the press about Tumblety and the Ripper connection he responded, 'There is no proof of his [Tumblety's] complicity in the Whitechapel murders and the crime for which he was under bond in London is not extraditable'. It is often referenced that Tumblety collected medical specimens, including uteri, but little evidence has been found to lay foundation to this claim, which was originally made by Colonel C.S. Dunham to the *Williamsport Sunday Grit* when he spoke of being a dinner guest when he had witnessed Tumblety fiercely denounce 'all women and especially fallen women'. He also went on to allege that Tumblety had then taken his guests to his office to show them twelve jars containing the uteri of every class of woman. These claims again break down very quickly because Dunham was a well-known confidence trickster and only made these claims after press allegations had made reference to Tumblety being involved with the Ripper murders. The strong likelihood is that he was making up stories to make a fast buck. So, can Tumblety be a reasonable suspect for the Ripper? The answer is no, his involvement is all rather weak and based on hearsay. As for being placed at the scene of the crimes, he certainly didn't match the descriptions given by the witnesses; in fact, there is absolutely no proof that he was even in Whitechapel at the time of the murders. There is no evidence that he was an aggressive man either. Littlechild even went as far as to say in his letter to Sims that Tunblety was, 'not known as a "sadist" [which the murderer unquestionably was]'. It has to be noted also that the police didn't suspect him, and remember, he had been released on bail for his prior arrest, and had they suspected him as the Ripper – even in the slightest bit – he'd have remained in custody. And it must be noted that if they suspected him after his release and subsequent departure to New York, they knew exactly where he was and could easily have got their counterparts to extradite him. With this all adding up against him, it is my belief that Dr Tumblety be removed from the suspect list.

James Maybrick

The Ripper Connection

James Maybrick, born on 24 October 1838, was a Liverpool cotton merchant and would seemingly have no connection to the case until 1992, when Michael Barrett, a former scrap metal merchant, put forward a journal that he alleged a friend of his, Tony Devereux, had given him in a pub in 1991. The diary was not named because a direct author was supposed to be a Liverpool cotton merchant by the name of James Maybrick. Maybrick had died in May 1889 of arsenic poisoning inflicted upon him by his wife, Florence, who was arrested and charged with murdering him. She was found guilty and sentenced to death, but after a cry of miscarriage of justice was proclaimed due to the persecution evidence being 'baffling' and a public outcry over the sentencing, her sentence was eventually reduced to life imprisonment before then being further reduced to 14 years. The diary claims that the author had witnessed his wife – who he would (rather unflatteringly) refer to as either 'the bitch', or 'the whore' within the pages – her with an unnamed lover in the Whitechapel area of Liverpool – this then would lead Maybrick to go on a murder spree in London. Very odd that he should commit five murders in a city with a district by the same name and some 212 miles apart from each other. The diary also contained long descriptions of the murders, ending with 'I give my name that all know of me. So history do tell. What love can do to a gentle man born. Yours truly. Jack the Ripper.' Maybrick was a completely new suspect when the journal surfaced in 1992. Did he write the diary or was it a hoax? Many are divided on the authenticity of it, though many others did agree that it appeared to correspond with the era nicely and most definitely could have been penned by Maybrick. The only way to prove its authenticity was through forensic analysis, but just as this was going through the motions, Michael Barrett confessed to forging the diary to the *Liverpool Post*. Surprisingly, he then retracted his confession and his ex-wife stated that the diary had been in her family's possession since the Second World War. The jury was now firmly out. So do the contents of the diary lead us to conclude that James Maybrick was the infamous fiend of Whitechapel? Put quite simply, not at all. An eager eye cast upon the diary will quickly ascertain that the contents appear to have been crafted from the press reports of the murders and accounts given by those asked at the time. This also quickly gives away all the mistakes made by the press at that time. One of the murders stands out more than the others, that of Mary Jane Kelly. The author describes with some glee how the body parts of the poor woman were spread around the room, but the body parts of Kelly were actually placed around the body, or at most within the close vicinity of her. Police reports clearly state this. They were definitely not cast around the room or 'hung like Christmas decorations' as the diary suggests. The diary claims her breasts, after being removed, were placed upon her bedside table, this is also a fallacy as they were discovered beneath her body. These claims alone strongly suggest that the author had not been at the scene but had instead just copied from articles and reports that added to the story rather than stated the true facts. Just as we prepare to close the case on Maybrick regarding the murders, a fascinating piece of memorabilia was discovered – an antique gold watch, purchased in 1993 by Albert Johnson. Upon inspecting it he found inside the scratched initials of the five Ripper victims together with the signature 'J. Maybrick' and the words, 'I am Jack'. The watch was sent for authentication and indeed was found to be circa 1888–1889 but the findings have been questioned and are still open to debate. What makes it questionable is the fact the watch was found in 1993, just a short time after the initial diary find. Could it be a coincidence or just another hoax thrown out to gain notoriety and financial gain? To have James Maybrick as a suspect is still open to debate and the authenticity of the diary and watch are key to the puzzle being solved. Until definitive evidence can be found, this particular suspect must stay on the list as a suspect.

Joseph Barnett

Joseph Barnett was born at 4 Hairbrain Court, Whitechapel on 25 May 1858. His parents, John and Catherine were Irish immigrants who had left Ireland during the Great Famine that had occurred between 1845 and 1852. They had a son, Denis, whilst in Ireland and upon their arrival in England, would go on to have a further four children Daniel, born 1851, Catherine, born 1853, Joseph, born 1858, and John, born 1860. John Snr worked as a porter at Billingsgate Fish Market and was to contract and die of pleurisy in July 1864 when Joseph was just 6 years old. From here, the eldest son, Denis, was to become the head of the house until he married Mary Ann Garrett and moved out of the family home to go and live at Bermondsey, on the other side of the River Thames. Joseph, like his father and brother, went to work at Billingsgate Fish Market as a porter and would do so for a decade before being sacked in October 1888 for stealing. Just before this he began living with Mary Jane Kelly. After her murder, little is known but we do know that he obtained another porter's licence at Billingsgate Market in 1906. At this time he lived with his brother, Daniel, at 18 New Gravel Lane, Shadwell. A year later he was residing at 60 Red Lion Street, Shadwell, and in 1908 at Tench Street, Wapping. In 1919 the electoral register shows he lived at 106 Red Lion Street, Shadwell, with a Louisa Barnett, who one would assume to be his wife, though there is nothing to say if they had any children. They remained at this address until Louisa died on 3 November 1926. Just 26 days later, Joseph was to pass away aged 68 of edema of the lungs and acute bronchitis.

The Ripper Connection

Barnett was roommates with Mary Jane Kelly until days before her murder on Friday, 9 November 1888. He had lost his job earlier in the year and this was the likely cause of Mary becoming a prostitute, although Barnett did find work in the construction industry. On 30 October he and Kelly had a violent altercation, which is believed to have been about his disapproval of the friends Kelly was keeping, i.e. prostitutes. During the night of the fight, objects had been thrown by the pair and a window beside the door had been broken. Barnett was to later state that despite their separation, they continued to see each other outside Miller's Court but only as friends. At this point, both would enter the property by putting their arm through the broken window to push the inner bolt to open the door, since they had lost the only key to the property and couldn't afford to have the lock replaced. Barnett would also admit to spending an hour with Kelly on the evening of her murder on 8 November. This was enough to gain suspicion amongst investigators and it is the first line of police investigation to suspect a spouse or former lover in such cases, even today. Despite Barnett stating that they would gain entry to Miller's Court via the broken window created during a fight, he also stated that the former couple remained on good terms with each other and had even secured a new job and gave financial help to Kelly. The case argued for his involvement wasn't made strongly until 1972, which is rather odd considering that Barnett ticks a great deal of boxes regarding the murders. The following are most striking:

1) Barnett may have had lied about the loss of the key to 13 Miller's Court after murdering Kelly.
2) The description of the murderer given virtually matches his appearance, including height and age.
3) He lived at the heart of Whitechapel.

The Suspects

4) An interesting theory is he may have met all the victims and known them quite well, which would explain why none of them seemingly fought back.
5) He admitted to having argued with Kelly the day before the murder.
6) It is postulated that Catherine Eddowes suspected Barnett to be the Ripper as she had allegedly told one person. As a witness it would make sense that she would be murdered.
7) Within the courtyard of Hanbury Street after the death of Annie Chapman, an envelope belonging to Barnett was found. Was this just coincidence or did Barnett drop the envelope from his pocket after killing Chapman?
8) Barnett originated from Ireland. The 'From Hell' letter sent to George Lusk was riddled with phasing indicative to Irish speaking people.
9) His job working as a fish porter would enable him to have the knives that inflicted the wounds on the victims.
10) Of note is the 'double event' of the night of 30 September. It has to be noted closely that the escape made by the killer led straight to Barnett's home. He could easily have washed his hands in the fountain that was near Miller's Court before he returned home.
11) At the scene of Mary Jane Kelly's murder, a tobacco pipe was found. Barnett stated he had left the abode they shared and taken with him all his belongings, yet the pipe was found at the crime scene.

Joseph Barnett is certainly a strong suspect in a classical sense as being the murderer and it was a tough call as to eliminate him, it is also surprising he wasn't considered strongly until 1972.

Seweryn Antonowicz Kłosowski/George Chapman

Seweryn Antonowicz Kłosowski was born on 14 December 1865 in Nagórna, Poland. He began an apprenticeship aged 14 to a senior surgeon, Moshko Rapport in Zwoleń, where he would aide Rapport in the application of leeches for blood letting, before he enrolling on a course of practical surgery at the Warsaw Praga Hospital, this course only lasted from October 1885 to January 1886 but he would continue to serve as a nurse or doctor's assistant until December 1886. He was to leave Poland shortly after and head for London. The exact timings are unclear, although hospital fees were discovered amongst his personal effects dated February 1887 so we can declare that he left for London shortly after this date. Once in England, he settled in the East End where he became a hairdresser's assistant in either late 1887 or early 1888, where he was employed by Abraham Radin at 70 West India Dock Road. His employment there was to last five months before he moved on to open his own shop at 126 Cable Street. This was also listed as his residence in the London directory of 1889. It was in 1889 that Kłosowski married a young Polish girl, Lucie Badewski, though he already had a wife in his native Poland. His wife learned of his second marriage and came to England to confront him but soon left to return to Poland. He and Lucie would have two children and move around various homes in London before moving to the United States in 1891 where they settled in Jersey City, New Jersey, where he found employment at a barbershop. All was not well in his marriage, and bitter fights would ensue, culminating in February 1892 when Kłosowski attacked Lucie while she was pregnant and threatened to kill her. Lucie returned to London and took residence with her sister where she would give birth to a daughter. Kłosowski would eventually return to London to reunite with Lucie before they would go their separate ways. In 1893 whilst working as an assistant in Haddin's hairdressers shop, Kłosowski would meet a woman named Annie Chapman (no relation to the Ripper victim) and began a relationship with her before moving in together. He also took her surname and from then on became known as George Chapman. After almost a year of living together, Chapman brought another woman to live with them, and Annie left a few weeks later whilst pregnant. In early 1895 she informed him of the pregnancy but he was not interested in offering any support to her. He would go on to take at least four mistresses who would pose as his wife; he was to murder three by poisoning them. Mary Isabella Spink (1858–1897); Bessie Taylor (died 22 October 1902); and Maud Marsh (died 22 October 1901).

His chosen method was to administer tartar emetic after buying it from a chemist in Hastings, Sussex. His reasons for killing the women are unclear apart from Spink, who had left him £500 in a legacy (equivalent to around £60,000 today). After Marsh died, suspicions surrounding her death led to the police investigating the death. Upon her body being exhumed, it was found that she had died by poisoning. Subsequently, the other two bodies were also exhumed and it became quickly evident that they too had fallen foul to the same method of despatch. Chapman was quickly arrested and charged with murder. He was to face prosecution by Sir Archibald Bodkin and the solicitor general, Sir Edward Carson, Chapman was convicted on 19 March 1903 and sentenced to death by hanging by Justice Grantham and was hung at Wandsworth Prison on 7 April 1903.

The Ripper Connection

Chapman's connection to the Ripper case began following his conviction for the aforementioned murders. The press quickly latched onto his case and a journalist from *The Pall Mall Gazette* hunted down the retired Inspector Frederick George Abberline. Abberline was quick to state that Chapman had never been a thought to him until the attorney general had made his opening statement at his trial. Abberline had apparently become 'so struck with the remarkable coincidences in the two series of murder' that he had not been able to think of anything else for several days past. The *Gazette* was to quote him that 'there are a score of things which make one believe Chapman is the man'. Some of these things included Chapman's study of surgery and that the Ripper murders were, in the words of Abberline, 'the work of an expert surgeon'. Abberline was also struck by the fact that Chapman arrived in England at the start of the murders and that also he lodged at George Yard, the location of the first murder. The murders ceased when Chapman went to America and 'similar murders began to be perpetuated in America after he landed there'. The problem with all of this, though it does appear to be very convincing, is that Abberline was wrong on several details. Chapman did have surgical training, but this is still a hotly debated factor even today regarding the Ripper; did he really have surgical skill? If you study the pathology of the victims, there is clearly no evidence of a surgeon performing his trade. A butcher, perhaps. Chapman's location and timing in the area is also of no great significance because, at that time, hundreds of people were doing exactly the same thing. The murders did end with his move to America, but this could have been pure coincidence. Finally, regarding the apparent similar American murders, no similar atrocities occurred. So, when all is said and done, was Chapman Jack the Ripper? Truthfully not. Though he was a convicted murderer, his MO was vastly different from that of the Ripper, who eviscerated his victims, and although a serial killer changing his MO certainly isn't unheard of, the fact that he went from barbaric mutilations to a mild-mannered form of murder in the shape of poisoning is definitely uncommon. George Chapman was a murderer of women but he was definitely not Jack the Ripper.

Michael Ostrog

Michael Ostrog was born in Russia around 1833 and little is known of his early years. He emigrated to England and first became known by the police in 1863 when he committed a robbery at the University of Oxford while using the alias of Max Grief. He would be arrested for this offence and end up serving a ten month jail sentence. Not learning his lessons, Ostrog was to be imprisoned the following year for three months for multiple frauds connected with the city of Cambridge. In December 1864, he was sentenced to eight months for fraud. In August 1866, he was jailed for a total of seven years after a series of robberies, which consisted mainly of the theft of gold watches from a jewellery store in Maidstone, Kent. Upon release from prison in 1873, Ostrog began a succession of thefts. He would be arrested and taken to the police station in Burton-upon-Trent, where he resisted and tried to fire a gun at the officers. In January 1874 he was convicted of a combination of robberies, contempt and attempted murder, and was sentenced to a total of ten years jail. He would be released in 1883. Four years later he was to steal a trophy from a cricket contest in July 1887. This would see him face a six month prison sentence. He was released in March 1888, and was considered 'cured' but an article in *The Police Gazette* described him as being very dangerous. Six months later, and this time in Paris, France, he again committed a robbery and was sentenced once more. He then left and returned to England where, in 1891, he was sent to an asylum in Surrey. After this, he would continue his ways of theft, scams and fraud, and would continue to be arrested and be contained in prisons until the year 1904, which is when any information on him ceases. It is presumed he died around this time, aged around 70–71. It is clear that Ostrog was a thief and fraudster who would dress to create new characters and would use numerous aliases to achieve his goals.

The Ripper Connection
Sir Melville Macnaghten identified Ostrog as a Ripper suspect in his memorandum, but the investigation didn't find any evidence of any violent crimes. There was definitely no sign of murder in his criminal past and, of course, as mentioned, he was arrested in France for a crime in 1888 and so has a clear-cut alibi so he could not be the Ripper.

Dr Thomas Neill Cream

Dr Cream was born in May 1850 in Scotland. The family were to emigrate to Canada in 1854 and we know that on 12 November 1872 Cream would register at McGill College in Montreal as a medical student, graduating with honours on 31 March 1876. He was to soon meet a Flora Elizabeth Brooks, the daughter of a wealthy hotel owner in Waterloo. She quickly fell pregnant and as the baby wasn't wanted, Cream took it upon himself to perform an abortion on her, a procedure that almost killed her. Her father was livid at this and demanded the couple marry, which they did on 11 September 1876. Cream left the next day for London where he would register as a graduate student at St Thomas's Hospital, London. Qualifications were also obtained from the Royal College of Physicians and Surgeons at Edinburgh. He then returned home to Canada after a few years and, despite his previous experience, began a new career as an abortionist. All seemed to be going well until the body of Kate Gardner, a chambermaid, was found in his office with a bottle of chloroform beside her. Surprisingly, Cream was not charged with murder, despite the obvious implications towards him. He would soon move to Chicago to open another practice. In August 1880, a Mary Anne Matilda Faulkner died surrounded by mysterious circumstances. This time Cream was arrested on charges of murder but was to evade conviction once more. As a side project, Cream created a concoction to help those suffering from epilepsy. The medicine seemed to work as he quickly gained a high reputation with people swearing his medicine was life changing. One such believer was Daniel Stott, who would send his wife, Julia, to Cream's office to acquire doses of the medicine on a regular basis. Cream and Stott's wife began an affair, which Stott eventually worked out and Cream was quick to add a bit of strychnine to his medicine. Stott was to die on 14 June 1881. The death was initially put down to epilepsy, but Cream wrote to the coroner to claim the pharmacist was responsible for the death, and asked for there to be an exhumation. Very strange behaviour from a person who had killed Stott. The coroner declined and dismissed the letter, but the district attorney overruled and had the body exhumed. Obviously strychnine was found within the stomach and Dr Cream's cup run finally came to an end. He was tried and convicted and sent to Illinois State Penitentiary to begin a life sentence. On 31 July 1891, he was released on good behaviour and quickly made his way to Canada, where he collected a $16,000 inheritance, before quickly leaving for England where he would wind-up in the South London slums. Just 48 hours after arriving, he met a prostitute called Matilda Clover whose fate was to die of nux vomica poisoning. Another woman, Ellen Donworth, would also die this way. Cream wasn't charged with either of these deaths. Two more women, Alice Marsh and Emma Shrivell, were to die next with Cream trying to extort money from a neighbour to the sum of £1,500, but the neighbour refused and Cream soon gave up on his attempt. Cream then stupidly would brag about the murders, including to a police sergeant who began surveillance on Cream and eventually he was arrested. He could run no more and was convicted of the death of Matilda Clover and sentenced to hang on 15 November 1892.

Poverty was so great in the East End of London at the time of the Ripper murders that people were forced to sleep outside. Seen here is a bench full of sleeping occupants, c.1900.

Church Street (now Fournier Street), Spitalfields, c.1900. This street ran parallel to Hanbury Street, where Annie Chapman was murdered. (Wellcome Collection)

High Street, Whitechapel, c.1850.

Dorset Street c.1902. Miller's Court, where Mary Jane Kelly was murdered, was accessed through an alleyway on the right.

Above: Poverty in the streets of Whitechapel. Wentworth Street, nineteenth century. (Wellcome Collection)

Opposite above: An image showing the queues that formed outside workhouses and how busy they were. This is Marylebone Workhouse, c.1900. (Wellcome Collection)

Opposite below: A casual ward for the poor, where Catherine Eddowes and Martha Tabram, for example, both spent time. This illustration being inside Marylebone Workhouse. (Wellcome Collection)

NEW WARD FOR THE CASUAL POOR AT MARYLEBONE WORKHOUSE.

WEST FRONT, OR PRINCIPAL ENTRANCE OF THE LONDON WORKHOUSE, BISHOPSGATE STREET.

Many of the Ripper's victims spent time in workhouses. This example is the City of London Workhouse, c.1819. (Wellcome Collection)

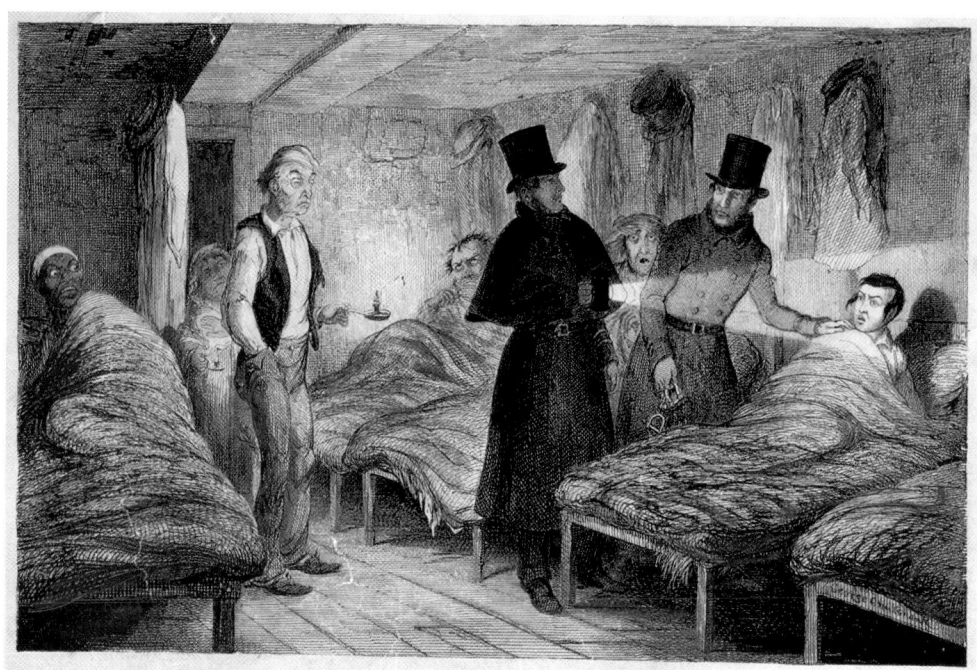

The victims were no strangers to a common lodging house. This image shows inside a shared bedroom in a three-penny lodging house, 1848. (Wellcome Collection)

This seems to be the only surviving photograph of Charles Allen Lechmere. It was reportedly taken in 1912, when he would have been around 63 years old.

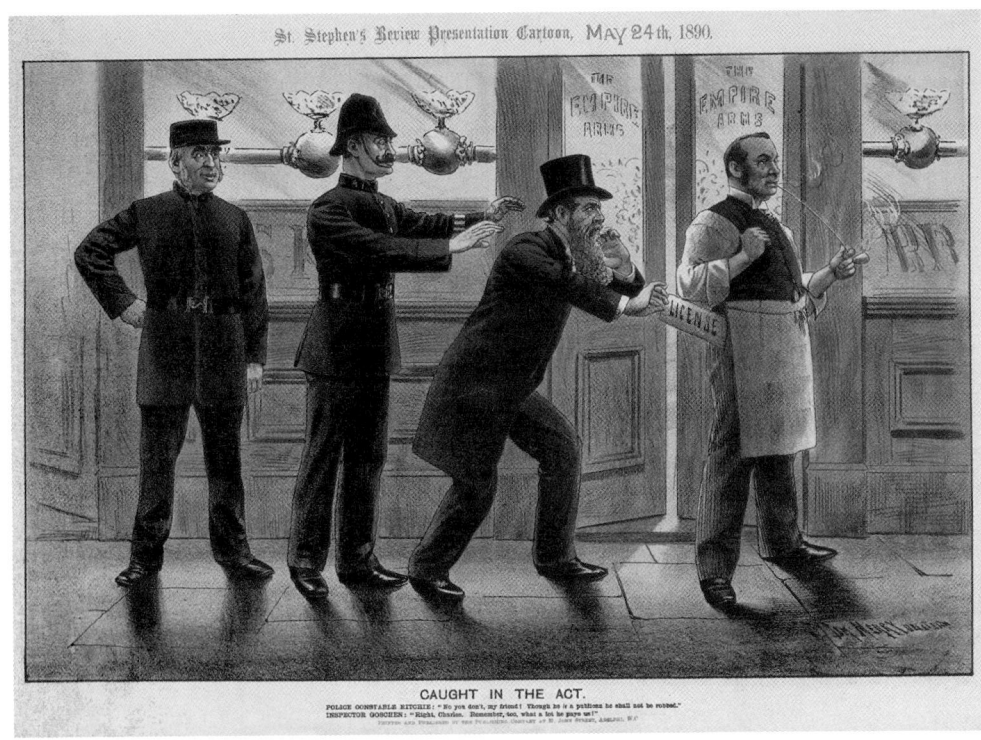

An illustration from 1890 depicting a police inspector (far left) and a police constable next to him, apprehending a pickpocket. The PCs who were on the scene at the Ripper murders will have been dressed in similar uniform on their beats. (Wellcome Collection)

The Ripper Connection
As the rope was placed and then tightened around his neck he exclaimed, 'I am Jack', and with the Ripper murders still a fresh memory in people's heads, it was instantly believed he was declaring himself to be Jack the Ripper. This was to be the only connection of Cream to the Whitechapel murders. Could Cream have been the Ripper? It is incredibly doubtful given that he was in prison at the time in America and also that his chosen MO was that of poisoning. Some did speculate that he had a double and that the prison guards were bribed and Cream was free to commit the crimes in Whitechapel. Although these claims are far-fetched they cannot be disproven. However, it is highly unlikely that Dr Cream was the Ripper and he can be easily eliminated from the list of suspects.

Prince Albert Victor

Everyone loves a royal conspiracy theory and the Ripper murders were no exception. The royal chosen to be put under fire in 1888 was the young Prince Albert Victor. Born 8 January 1964, as the grandson of Queen Victoria, he was second in line to the throne. For one with such privilege in his life and clearly a bold and safe future compared to his future subjects, things would go very wrong for him. Prince Albert was regarded as a disappointment to the royal family, due to an inadequate military career and rumoured reports of homosexuality. With such a complex character, much speculation followed him in his later years, although it must be remembered that he died in 1892, aged just 28.

The Ripper Connection
Could a prince, second to the throne, really be responsible for the slaughter of the unfortunate area of Whitechapel? The actual theory of the prince being the Ripper didn't come to light until 1962 in a book written by Philippe Jullian. Jullian's claim that Prince Albert Victor was the Ripper was by far a bold one. Shortly afterwards an article was written by Dr Thomas Stowell where he too claimed Victor to be the Ripper based

entirely upon the findings of Prince Victor's doctor, Sir William Gull. It all made for a great story that appealed greatly to those needing fresh food for thought on the case, but no actual proof was forthcoming and, with this, the theory could never really take a hold. One fact was clear though – Prince Albert's state of mind. Dr Stowell stated that the young prince contracted syphilis in the West Indies and that the disease led to a rapid decline in his mental health and would eventually cause him to become insane and this insanity was to lead him to commit the murders. Stowell would also go on, saying that the royal family were fully aware of his mental health and his secured double life as Jack the Ripper. He claimed that the royal family also chose to do nothing about this. The syphilis took a stronger hold on his mental health and he was eventually confined to an asylum where he lived out the remainder of his days. This all sounds plausible, but again there is absolutely no definitive evidence to back the claim. An example is Stowell's claim of using Gull's medical notes on the prince. Remember, the murders were committed in 1888, Gull died in 1890 and Prince Victor died in 1892. Further research shows that Prince Victor wasn't even in London during the majority of the Whitechapel murders. A later theory postulated that one of the Whitechapel victims was pregnant with the prince's child. It was put forward that the Jack the Ripper murders were created to silence her and protect the integrity of the royal family. No evidence has ever come to light to support this theory. With all this said and done, it is again certain that Prince Albert Victor, despite his many problems, was not the murderer and can be taken off the list, just for the lack of concrete evidence against him and the fact he wasn't even in London for at least two of the murders.

William Henry Bury

William Henry Bury was born on 25 May 1859 at Stourbridge, Worcestershire. At an early age he was orphaned and was educated at a charitable school in the Midlands. After leaving school he found regular employment in the area but fell into financial troubles a few years later and was sacked from his job for theft, becoming a street peddler. His whereabouts after this are not known but it appears he lived an unsettled life in the Midlands and Yorkshire areas. In October 1887 we know he arrived in Bow, London, where he was to find work selling sawdust for James Martin, who it appears also operated a brothel at 80 Quickett Street, Bow. Bury lived in the stables but later moved into the house where he met Ellen Elliot, who Martin employed as a servant, and she was more than likely a prostitute there. Ellen was born in Walworth, London, on 24 October 1856. Her father ran the Bricklayer's Arms pub. Ellen began her working life as a needlewoman. In 1883 she had an illegitimate daughter who was to die aged 2 in December 1885. Within a year she began working for Martin. In March of 1888, Ellen and Bury left Martin's employ and moved to a furnished room at 3 Swaton Road, Bow, where they lived until they got married on Easter Monday, 2 April 1888, at Bromley Parish Church. It was later revealed by Martin that he had dismissed Bury because of unpaid debts. At 3 Swaton Road, the landlady, Elizabeth Haynes, described Bury as a violent drunk (something Martin attested to also). On 7 April 1888, just five days into their marriage, Haynes caught Bury kneeling on his wife and threatening to cut her throat with a knife. Haynes subsequently evicted them and they found their way back to Martin after the debt was paid off by Ellen. Martin employed Bury once more and the couple moved to 11 Blackthorn Street, which is close to Swaton Road. Martin would then claim that Bury had developed venereal disease. Ellen then sold her remaining five £100 railway company shares that she had inherited from an aunt, and in August, the couple moved to 3 Spanby Road. The money they got from the shares was also spent on week's holiday to Wolverhampton where they binge drank and Ellen was also to buy jewellery. Bury was still assaulting his wife and would continue to do so for the rest of the year. As December began, Ellen had all but ran out of money, so Bury was forced to sell his horse and cart. In January 1889 he would inform the landlord at Spanby Road that he was thinking of moving abroad and emigrate to Brisbane, Australia. Bury and Ellen were to eventually end up in Dundee, Scotland. Ellen wasn't keen on the move but after Bury had secured a job in a factory she agreed to go. They were to arrive in Dundee on 20 January 1889 and the following day rented a room above a bar at 43 Union Street. Eight days later they moved out and moved to a squat at 113 Prince's Street in a basement flat under a shop. Bury continued to drink heavily and befriended a painter named David Walker. Things began to take a more sinister turn when, on 14 February, Bury bought some rope at his local grocer's shop before spending the rest of the day watching closely at the sheriff court from the public gallery. He did this again on the 7th, and on the 10th he visited his friend, Walker, who lent him a newspaper that contained an article on a woman's suicide by hanging.

The Ripper Connection
That evening Bury walked into the central police station in Dundee to report the suicide of his wife by hanging. He said that after a night of heavy drinking he had woken to find his wife with a rope around her neck. Bury hadn't called for a doctor but instead had cut the body and hidden it in one of the packing cases brought up from London. He then told the officer he was afraid his actions would lead to his arrest and him being accused of being the Ripper. The police went to his flat and indeed found the mutilated body of Ellen. They returned to the station and found, in Bury's possession, a small knife, a key, and Ellen's jewellery. One interesting thing found at the flat was graffiti on the rear door of which read 'Jack Ripper [sic] is at the back of this door' and on the stairwell more was found reading 'Jack Ripper is in this seller [sic]'. Eventually Bury was convicted of his crime and sentenced to death. He was hanged on 24 April 1889.

Bury's connection to the Ripper comes from newspapers. After the time of his arrest, it became apparent he had inflicted mutilations on the young woman's body, just as the Ripper had done. The press also latched onto the fact Bury had lived in Bow, near to Whitechapel. *The New York Times* went as far as to directly name him as the Ripper and further claimed that he had killed his wife because she knew his true identity. *The Dundee Courier & Argus* picked up on this the following day. Bury's executioner, James Berry, also went as far as to say Bury was indeed the Ripper. Strangely, Berry never mentioned this in his memoirs,

My Experiences as an Executioner by Ernest A. Parr, a journalist located in Newmarket, but Suffolk wrote to the secretary of state for Scotland on 28 March 1908 that Berry in his words 'told me explicitly that Bury was known to have been Jack the Ripper'. A few others over the following decades began to believe Bury to be the Ripper, noting how he took his wife's rings, mutilated her body as the Ripper had done and also how the murders ceased as he left for Dundee. It has to be remembered that Ellen was strangled before Bury mutilated her body, whereas the Ripper cut the throats of his victims before eviscerating them. So there are only limited similarities between the two. I believe that Bury was a violent drunk who certainly showed his aggression to his wife and ultimately murdered her. Did he have it in him to be the Ripper? Yes, he did, but because of his lack of previous convictions or violence towards others. A murderer he was. Jack the Ripper he was not.

Nathan Kaminsky/David Cohen

David Cohen is a name mentioned in the case of Jack the Ripper on a regular basis, but little is known of him. His name was first proposed by the late greatly respected author and Ripperologist Martin Fido, who was initially researching the London public asylum records between 1888 and 1890. Fido was specifically looking for a man named Kosmiński but couldn't find anyone by that name and instead came across a man named David Cohen who appeared to fill many of the gaps that Macnaghten, Swanson and Anderson were unable to. We know he was born in 1865 and thus was around 23 at the time of the murders. By description, we know he had both brown hair and eyes, as well as a beard. In early December of 1888, he lived at 86 Leman Street and was found wandering around the streets and talking little but what he did say was in Yiddish. He was taken to a police station where it was determined that because he could not care for himself, he would be taken to a local workhouse. It wasn't long before he became violent and was escorted there under restraint. Upon arrival he was placed in the infirmary where he was given the name

David Cohen, which was the modern day equivalent of 'John Doe'. While in the infirmary he continued to be violent and noisy and was considered a danger to others. On 21 December he was, under restraint, taken to Colney Hatch Asylum, where his occupation was given as a tailor. Here, the extent of his violent behaviour became such that he was separated from the other inmates. Under constant supervision in the asylum he was described as 'spiteful and mischievous'. He would spit out food, he would kick passers-by and rip down a pipe and window guard. He would only live until October 1889, when he died as a result of 'exhaustion of mania'.

The Ripper Connection

As we learned, David Cohen was not his real name, and it is speculated that his real name was Nathan Kaminsky. Kaminsky was a Polish Jew who matched the description of the man nicknamed 'leather apron'. Sir Robert Anderson, who was the assistant commissioner in CID at Scotland Yard during the time of the murders, wrote in 1895 that the killer had been identified by a witness who was unwilling to come forward, 'the only person who had ever had a good view of the murderer unhesitatingly identified the suspect the instant he was confronted with him; but he refused to give evidence against him'. In an article titled 'The Lighter Side of My Official Life', published in 1910, Anderson included a memoir hand-written by ex-Superintendent (chief inspector at the time of the Ripper murders) Donald Sutherland Swanson, in which he named Aaron Kosmiński as the man who matched the description of the Polish Jew. It read as follows:

> The suspect had, at the Seaside Home where he had been sent by us with difficulty in order to subject him to identification, and he knew he was identified. On the suspects return to his brother's house in Whitechapel he was watched by the police (city CID) day and night. In time, the suspect with his hands tied behind his back, he was sent to Stepney Workhouse and then to Colney Hatch and died shortly afterwards – Kosmiński was the suspect – DSS.

It would now appear that we have a case of mistaken identity because we know that Kosmiński died in 1919, so he could not have been the suspect who had died shortly after arriving at Colney Hatch, some nine years after Anderson's book. Martin Fido linked him because the timings worked well and Kaminsky was known to be living in the Black Lion Yard, which was close to the murders. As Sir Robert Anderson wrote, 'One did not need to be a Sherlock Holmes to discover that the criminal was a sexual maniac of a virulent type, that he was living in the immediate vicinity of the scenes of the murders'. We can also say that Aaron Kosmiński was far from a violent person but Cohen/Kaminsky certainly was. Nobody can say for sure if Nathan Kasminsky/David Cohen was the Ripper. Evidence is very scant regarding him but one thing for sure is that he certainly had the capabilities to be the Ripper.

Thomas Hayne Cutbush

Thomas Hayne Cutbush, born on 29 June 1866 only a few miles from Whitechapel, was named as a possible Ripper suspect at the time.

The Ripper Connection
Cutbush is no longer widely considered a serious suspect for the Ripper killings for several reasons, which include his mental instability, his location during the murders and lack of hard evidence against him.

His mental illness included delusions and erratic behaviour, which at the time fitted the crime has to be questioned today because crimes as intricate as these would need a person with a clear mind for planning such sophisticated murders.

His location at the time of the murders was outside of the area of Whitechapel making it difficult to tie him in with the locations and especially with an escape due to his mental state. A person suffering with his conditions would make a mistake and be apprehended quickly.

And finally, there was no evidence found against him and although the police did investigate him, it quickly became apparent that his profile did not match the one of Jack the Ripper. This said, I believe we can rule him out of the case.

James Kelly

James Kelly was born in Preston on 20 April 1860. His mother, Sarah Kelly, left him to be brought up by his grandmother, Therese. Although his start in life was a hard one, he was bequeathed the sum of £20,000, which he was able to collect upon reaching the age of 25. In 1878 he began work as an upholsterer and would move around amongst various employers in his job. In 1880 he met an 18-year-old woman named Sarah Brider and the pair moved into her parental home. He initially came across as a good-mannered religious man (the Brider family were devout Catholics), but it was here that Kelly began to show an unpredictable nature and an even more alarming explosive temper. This would eventually cause Kelly to lose his job. Just a few days later he was to marry Sarah on 4 June 1883. Instead of a happy union though, Kelly would display bouts of obsessive jealousy, accusing his wife of affairs, even believing she had a sexually transmitted disease. On 21 June 1883, just seventeen days into the marriage, Kelly slashed the throat of his wife with a knife after a violent argument. He offered no resistance upon arrest and on 24 June, Sarah died of her injuries. He was charged with aggravated homicide the following day. Due to his mental state, a coroner had to declare him fit for trial. Lawyers appealed and petitions were signed but ultimately Kelly was sentenced to death by hanging and the date was set for 20 August 1883. On 7 August, Dr W. Orange, superintendent of the Broadmoor Hospital, examined Kelly and declared him to be insane. Mr Hiron, a former boss of Kelly's, also attested to his 'abnormal attitude' and with that the death sentence was quashed and a sentence of indefinite confinement to the asylum was handed down. Despite his state of mind, Kelly was regarded as a model inmate, but on 23 January 1888 he escaped from Broadmoor using a key he'd made by modelling a piece of metal. A warrant was issued for his arrest. On 10 November 1888, the day of the murder of Mary Jane Kelly, the police made a search of the home of Sarah Brider's parents but they didn't find him there. Kelly was at large for decades until on 12 February 1927 he turned himself in at Broadmoor, some 39 years after his escape. He begged to be readmitted and allegedly told a local newspaper, 'I am very tired and I want to die with my friends'. He was to live there for two years before he died on 17 September 1929 of double lobar pneumonia.

The Ripper Connection

For the last two years of his life, Kelly wrote memoirs that were found by a police investigator, Ed Norris. The memoirs express a hatred for prostitutes and he wrote that he had hidden in London between the months of August and November 1888, which coincides nicely with the time of all the murders. It later turned out that Kelly had escaped to America and after some copycat murders there, a link was formulated that the murderer was a psychotic escapee from Broadmoor. Carrie Brown was murdered in the room of a New York hotel on 24 April 1891 and was considered a potential victim of the Ripper. Upon his return to England in 1927, Kelly was now 67 years old with ailing health issues and would say of his time in America that he had devoted himself to 'fighting against evil'. Kelly most certainly had the characteristics to be the Ripper but connecting him to the Whitechapel murders is almost impossible to do. He is most definitely a very interesting character though and worthy of making the list.

Sir John Williams

Sir John Williams was born on 6 November 1840 in Gwynfe Hamlet, Carmarthenshire. He was schooled in Swansea before going to the University of Glasgow and then on to University College Hospital, London, where he completed his medical studies. He was to be knighted after a visit to King Edward VII at Sandringham House on 29 December 1902. He appears to have had a fairly ordinary life where he spent most of his spare time collecting books and paintings all from rural life in Wales. He married Mary Hughes in 1872 but there were no children from the marriage.

The Ripper Connection

The accusation of his Ripper involvement came in a 2005 book, *Uncle Jack*, which was written by one of his distant relatives. The book suggests that the victims all knew the doctor personally, and that they were killed and eviscerated as an attempt to research the cause of infertility. Also mentioned was that a badly blunted surgical knife that had belonged to Sir John was the knife used in the crimes. These accusations and claims have become seriously doubted, however, and the Ripper is very unlikely to have been Sir John.

George Hutchinson

Very little is known of George Hutchinson. He was described as an unemployed labourer and former groom who lived in the Victoria Home for Working Men on Commercial Street. Even the press reports at the time couldn't give his age; it was reported to be somewhere between 22 and 33 years, with some claiming he'd served within the British Army, though no rank was given or confirmed.

The Ripper Connection

Hutchinson's connection stems from an eyewitness account he gave the police on 12 November 1888, three days after the murder of Mary Jane Kelly. He went into the Commercial Street Police Station where a statement was taken by Sergeant Edward Badham. Hutchinson claimed he'd seen Kelly just hours before her death in the company of a client who apparently was too elegant for an area like Whitechapel. He stated that at 2 am on the morning of 9 November he was walking along Commercial Street on his way home, and on Flower and Dean Street he saw Kelly. She greeted him by name and asked him for a sixpence. Hutchinson couldn't oblige as he'd already spent all his money during the evening. She then said that she needed to find some money and began to walk towards Thrawl Street. Within seconds, a man approaching from the opposite direction to Kelly tapped her upon the shoulder and whispered something into her ear; possibly a joke as both then laughed. Hutchinson said that he heard the man say, 'You will be alright for what I have told you'. He then put his right arm on Kelly's shoulder and they both hugged. Hutchinson

The Suspects

also noted the man was carrying 'a kind of a small parcel in his left hand with a kind of scrap round it'. Hutchinson said he paid a lot of attention to Mary's client because of his 'Jewish appearance' along with the elegant clothes he was wearing which made him stick out like a sore thumb in such a poor area. Hutchinson then made his way to the gas lamp that lit the entrance to the Queen's Head Tavern, so that he could use it to take a closer look at proceedings between the mysterious man and Kelly. According to Hutchinson, he bent down to take a look at the man's face, the pair then headed to Dorset Street, with Hutchinson following who said he saw them talk for three minutes before the duo entered Miller's Court, where Kelly lived. The man with Kelly then whispered something to her to which she replied, 'come, I will make you feel comfortable, dear'. After that he hugged and kissed her. Before they entered her dwelling, Kelly stopped and told the man that she lost her handkerchief, the man then took out his own red handkerchief and gave it to her. They entered the courtyard whereupon Hutchinson could no longer continue spying, so he chose to wait outside for forty-five minutes. Neither were seen by Hutchinson during this time and he decided to leave. When asked to give a description of the man, Hutchinson said,

'[Age] about 34 or 35. Height 5ft 6, complexion pale, dark eyes and eyelashes, slight moustache, curled up each end, and hair dark, very surly looking dress, long dark coat, collar and cuffs trimmed astrakhan [sic]. And a dark jacket under, light waistcoat, dark trousers [and a] dark felt hat turned down in the middle. Button boots and gaiters with white buttons. Wore a very thick gold chain, white linen collar. Black tie with horse shoe pin. Respectable appearance, walked very sharp. Jewish appearance. Can be identified.' A woman named Sarah Lewis later said that she had seen Hutchinson loitering around the building where Kelly stayed. Inspector Abberline even interrogated Hutchinson in person and would later tell the media that he believed Hutchinson's account to be the truth, believing him to be sincere. Hutchinson spoke to the press also, stating that on 10 November, the day after Kelly's murder, he had gone out searching for the man he'd seen and actually found him and began following him, but the man had seen Hutchinson and quickened his pace, eventually evading him by escaping through the streets of Spitalfields. Hutchinson never saw him again. Hutchinson further said,

> I went down to the Shoreditch mortuary today and recognised the body as being that of the woman Kelly, whom I saw at two o'clock on Friday morning. Kelly did not seem to me to be drunk, but was a little bit spreeish. After I left the court I walked about all night, as the place where I usually sleep was closed. I was able to fix the time, as it was between ten and five minutes to two o'clock as I came by Whitechapel Church. When I left the corner of Miller's Court the clock struck three o'clock. One policeman went by the Commercial Street end of Dorset Street while I was standing there, but no one came down Dorset Street. I saw one man go into a lodging house in Dorset Street, and no one else, I have been looking for the man all day.

This is a truly amazing statement to give to the police because Hutchinson had virtually heard and seen everything apart from the actual murder of Mary Jane Kelly. Given the circumstances of the night in question, one can only imagine that his sight and hearing were virtually perfect in every way, but was he telling the truth? He had either made up an elaborate story or he had given us the best possible description of Jack the Ripper. He could also have delivered his statement but the facts had been given artistic licence by the police and press or perhaps the statement was lies and a distraction because he was the Ripper and a witness had seen him, namely Sarah Lewis. Other options could be that he intended to rob the well-dressed man because he was broke. Was he hanging around until the morning because he couldn't afford lodgings and to also keep out of the weather? Or, of course, he was genuinely worried for Kelly's safety because he had known her for three years and with a killer woman of the night out on the streets, he wanted to protect her. One slight oddity with Hutchinson's story was that he claimed the man was too well-dressed for the area but later said, 'I believe he lives in the area'. This leads on to another question: would the Ripper not just wear the clothes of the average working man? But that is a question for later on.

The all important question, however, is, was George Hutchinson Jack the Ripper? He definitely knew one of the victims by name and confessed to giving her money on occasions, so perhaps he was a regular client? We also know he was one of the last people to see her alive. We know his address, the Victoria Home for Working Men located at 39–41 Commercial Street, at the very heart of he Ripper's hunting ground, and that it took him three days to come forward with his statement, a dubious statement at that given the remarkable detail given. Had he, in fact, been seen by Sarah Lewis and panicked and taken three days to come up with such a remarkable story? He told police he entered the courtyard yet told the press he waited outside of Kelly's window. It's indeed odd that this discrepancy in his statements wasn't picked up on. George Hutchinson was never to be heard of again but the story doesn't end just yet. Melvyn Fairclough interviewed Reginald Hutchinson for his book *The Ripper and the Royals*. Hutchinson claimed his father, George William Topping Hutchinson (1866–1938), was the man who knew Kelly. A date of birth given as 1 October 1866 made him 22 at the time of the murders and he was described as an honest, hard-working plumber who was always at work. He also stated his father could remember great details accurately. He had told his son he'd been spoken to by police and when Reginald asked his father who the Ripper was, he replied, 'It was more to do with the royal family than ordinary people'. Reginald also said his father received 100 shillings, though would not reveal why such a substantial amount of money was given to him. A strange coincidence is that Hutchinson's police description bore a striking resemblance to Lord Randolph Churchill. Surprisingly there was other witness accounts of the Ripper given. J. Best of 82 Lower Chapman Street described a man who was in the company of Elizabeth Stride on the night she was murdered and gave the following statement:

> I was in the Bricklayer's Arms, Settles-Street, about two hundred yards from the scene of the murder on Saturday night, shortly

before eleven, and saw a man and a woman in a doorway. They had been served in the public house and went out when me and my friends came in. It was raining very fast, and they did not appear willing to go out. He was hugging her and kissing her, and as he seemed a respectably dressed man, we were rather astonished at the way he was going on with the woman, who was poorly dressed. We 'chipped' him, but he paid no attention. As he stood in the doorway, he always threw sidelong glances into the bar, but would look nobody in the face. I said to him, 'why don't you bring the woman in and treat her?' But he gave no answer. If he had been a straight fellow he would have told us to mind our own business, or he would have gone away. I was so certain that there was something up that I would have charged him if I could have seen a policeman. When the man could not stand the chaffing any longer he and the woman went off like a shot soon after eleven. I had been to the mortuary, and am almost certain that the woman there is the one we saw at the Bricklayer's Arms. She is the same slight woman, and seems the same height. The face looks the same, but a little paler, and the bridge of the nose does not look so prominent.'

It appears that Hutchinson's description was not as far-fetched as once thought. It must also be remembered that Hutchinson was rewarded for his dealings with both police and press, another potential reason for so much help perhaps? Although, as a suspect, George Hutchinson is a compelling candidate to be the Ripper, it was more likely that he was just out for quick cash and time in the spotlight.

Charles Allen Cross/Lechmere

We'll discuss this suspect in further detail later in the book.

CHAPTER 9

Why Didn't the Author of Sherlock Holmes Enter the Case?

Sir Arthur Conan Doyle is, of course, today world-known for his Sherlock Holmes crime mysteries but did he ever chip in to the investigation, and if not, why not? With such a clinical mind as his, Doyle must have pondered the case in his study whilst concocting his latest Holmes story. *A Study in Scarlet* was released in 1887 but it wasn't until 1890 that *The Sign of the Four* was published. and *The Adventures of Sherlock Holmes* series followed in 1892, so there was time for him to incorporate the Ripper into his stories, but he didn't. The logical explanation for this is that it was all very raw at the time and that being seen to exploit the population for financial gain would be a damning thing to do for one's career. It would have been seen as incredibly disrespectful and a possible analogy of today would be an author writing about 9/11 in their fiction a year or so after the event. That said, the author Diane Madsen said that Doyle and his mentor, Dr Joseph Bell, actually independently named the Ripper. Allegedly, Bell had said he had a friend (Doyle) who liked puzzles and that they had both researched the Whitechapel murders. After they had finished their research, they both wrote their suspect down and sealed it in an envelope, which they then exchanged – both envelopes contained the same name independently. Bell is said by Madsen to have filed a report to Scotland Yard and then the murders ceased immediately. Madsen believes that both men suspected James K. Stephen who was a tutor to Prince Albert Victor, son of the Prince of Wales. So, with two such esteemed minds allegedly coming to the same conclusion. I think it to be only fitting that our final potential suspect should be the one that they independently came to.

James Kenneth Stephen

Born in London in 1859, Stephen was the second son of Sir James Fitzjames Stephen, a barrister-at-law and his wife Mary Richards Cunningham, and was a first cousin to Virginia Woolf (one of the most important modernist writers of the twentieth century). Stephen studied at Eton College. He gained a reputation as an intellectual and apparently spoke in a pedantic, but highly articulate and entertaining, manner, At King's College, Cambridge he was said to have had a fantastic academic career and became a member of the Apostles Intellectual Society, before becoming President of the Cambridge Union Society in the Michaelmas term of 1880, and a Fellow of King's College in 1885. He became a tutor and companion of Prince Albert Victor. His role was to boost the poor academic standard the prince displayed. Initially, Stephen was confident he could bolster the prince's standards, but before they were to move to Trinity College, Cambridge, Stephen would concede; 'I do not think he can possibly derive much benefit from attending lectures at Cambridge... He hardly knows the meaning of the words to read'.

At this point, it has to be noted that the writer Micheal Harrison in 1972 claimed that Stephen and the prince were in a sexual relationship that would conclude when the prince was gazetted to the 10th Hussars on 17 June 1885, and resulted in a Royal Scandal, though little evidence of this is evidence today. On 29 December 1886, while on a short break in Felixstowe, Suffolk with his friend Felix Cobbold, Stephen sustained a serious head injury. The accident was either caused by an object striking him on the head from a moving train, or he was injured when a horse he was riding shied and backed him into the moving vane of a windmill. The physical scars healed quickly but mentally, he was never the same again, displaying erratic emotional and mental episodes, which certainly only worsened his bipolar disorder. The biographer of his cousin,

Virginia Woolf, Quentin Bell once told the story of Stephen thrusting a sword blade into some bread, suffering delusions that he was a painter of immense genius. Stephen would also rush around in a hansom cab and 'on another occasion he appeared at breakfast and announced, as though it were an amusing incident, that the doctors had told him that he would either die or go completely mad'. Stephen would shortly become a patient of Sir William Gull. His mental and physical health would quickly decline and apart from composing two volumes of poetry, he had no focus on any other project he started. He was quickly then committed to an asylum for the insane.

The Ripper Connection
The notion that Stephen could be involved was first postulated in 1970 by Thomas E.A. Stowell after researching papers left by Sir William Gull. It was an alleged theory, but in 1972, Micheal Harrison working on Stowell's theory, deduced that 'S', written in Gull's notes was not a reference to Prince Albert Victor but the 'S' actually was referring to Stephen. Harrison purported that Stephen had committed the Whitechapel murders 'out of a twisted desire for revenge', because of the alleged dissolving of a homosexual relationship between Stephen and the prince. He continued that the failing of the relationship, coupled with Stephen's mental decline, made Stephen act out one of the poems he'd written called 'Air' and 'Kafoozalum', in which the leading character kills ten prostitutes. David Abrahamsen, a forensic psychiatrist, has also linked the profile of Stephen to that of Jack the Ripper and suggested that Stephen and the prince worked together and that Stephen was the leader. The claim falls flat easily though as Stephen was in a similar situation to Druitt, in that after committing the crime, Stephen would have had to return to Cambridge for lectures the following day. Connections were made to Stephen's writing style and that of the Ripper letters but this was quickly disproved.

Chapter 10

Potential Other Ripper Victims

Rose Mylett

On Wednesday, 19 December 1888, Charles Ptolomey was walking along England Row, just off Poplar High Street, and saw a woman with two sailors at the entrance to Clarke's Yard. Ptolomey said one of the sailors was around 5 feet 11 inches tall and, according to Ptolomey, 'looked like a yankee' and the other was said to have been 5 feet 7 inches tall. Ptolomey saw the shorter one talking with the woman who he later was to confirm was Rose Mylett after he went to see her body at the mortuary. Ptolomey noted that the taller man walked up and down as the shorter man spoke to Mylett. Ptolomey found the behaviour of the two sailors odd, to the point that he told the *Daily Chronicle* that, 'I stopped and took account of them'. The woman then allegedly said to the shorter one 'No, no, no!' before the man spoke to her in a lower tone. Ptolomey continued, 'it struck me that they were there for a good purpose … and that was the reason I took so much notice of their movements. I shall always remember their faces, and I could pick them out of a thousand'. Mylett was also reportedly perfectly sober. Ptolomey had seen this at 7.55 pm on the 19th, and at 4.30 am on the morning of 20 December, Sergeant Robert Golding and Police Constable Thomas Costello were to come across her dead body in Clarke's Yard. The body was still warm, which, given the time of year, indicated that she hadn't been dead long. What we know is that two hours prior to her body being found, Alice Graves had seen Mylett still in the company of the two men, but this time Mylett was drunk. A report by Metropolitan Police commissioner, James Monro, stated 'the face was perfectly placid. The clothes were not disarranged and round the neck was a handkerchief loosely folded, but not tied. In the pocket of the dress was a small phal empty. In one of the ears was an earring, the other was missing'. No indication of a fight or defensive wounds were seen. The police initially believed she'd died from either suicide or natural causes. Police surgeon Dr George James Harris was summoned, and after an examination of her body, on which he found no marks, or even any sign of her being murdered, he declared life to be extinct and that the body was to be removed to the mortuary. Upon arrival at the mortuary, the mortuary keeper and coroner's assistant, Curtain T. Chives, found a mark around her neck, which was 1/8th of an inch deep, with some scratches above it. With the evidence now looking like foul play was at hand, a post mortem was arranged. This was carried out on 21 December by divisional police surgeon Dr Matthew Brownfield and his findings were as follows:

> Blood was oozing from the nostrils, and there was a slight abrasion on the right side of her face. On the neck was a mark which had evidently been caused by cord drawn tightly round the neck, from the spine to the left ear. Such a mark would have been by a four-thread cord. There were also impressions of the thumbs and middle index fingers of some person plainly visible on each side of the neck... Death was due to strangulation. Deceased could not have done it by herself. Marks on her neck were probably caused by her trying to pull the cord off. Murderer must have stood at the left rear of the woman, and, having the ends of the cord round his hands, thrown it round her throat, crossed his hands and thus strangled her...

Then came an embarrassing situation of the police not being aware of Dr Brownfield's findings and thus they still believed that Mylett had died with no foul play involved no investigation was launched with Monro having to concede: 'This evidence was certainly a matter of surprise to the police, but accepting the medical evidence as correct, the case was clearly one of murder…' He also confessed that he himself had been caught out by her 'perfect placid features' and the 'absence of all signs of violence when the body was discovered'. Monro asked for a second opinion from surgeon Mr Mackellar who agreed with Brownfield's findings that death was via strangulation. Monro was to say 'there is therefore no doubt that the case was one of murder – and murder of a strange and unusual type'. With five weeks passing since the last confirmed Ripper murders, police and press were eager to dampen down any fears that were spreading through the locals of Whitechapel. Coroner Wynne Baxter stated at the inquest that, 'the usual signs of strangulation, such as protrusion of the tongue and clenching of the hands, were absent, there being nothing all suggestive of death by violence'. The jury were to return a verdict of 'murder by person, or persons unknown'.

Was Rose Mylett a Ripper Victim?

Everything indicates that she probably wasn't a victim and most experts agree, but the truth can never been known for sure.

Alice McKenzie

Alice McKenzie was born in 1849 in what was believed to be Peterborough. Little, if anything, is known about her early life but from 1883. We know she was living on and off with John McCormack at various lodging houses in the East End. From April 1889, the couple lived mainly at Mr Tenpenny's common lodging house, 52 Gun Street, Spitalfields. McCormack was born in around 1826 and was an Irish porter who had worked in casual work for Jewish tailors in Hanbury Street for about sixteen years. He met Alice at Bishopsgate. He said he'd seen McKenzie at 4 am on 16 July 1889 when he'd returned from work and before going to sleep he'd given her 1s/8d. When he awoke at between 10 and 11 am, he noted McKenzie had gone out and he wasn't to see her again until he was to identify her body at the mortuary the following afternoon. At 12.50 am, 17 July 1889, Police Constable Walter Andrews found the body of Alice McKenzie lying beside a lamppost on a pavement in Castle Alley, just off Whitechapel High Street. Her skirt was pulled up and blood was evident over her thigh and abdomen, which was coming from a zigzag superficial wound that originated just beneath her left breast and ran down to her navel. Her identity wasn't known at first and a description was released to the press, with the *Western Times* publishing the following description on Thursday, 18 July 1889:

> The victim of the murder was about forty-five years of age, and was about five foot four inches in height, she had brown hair and eyes and a fair complexion. She is believed to have been of the 'unfortunate' class, but has not yet been identified. She wore a red staff bodice, patched under the arm and a brown staff skirt. She also had on a linsey petticoat, black stockings, buttoned boots, and a paisley shawl, but no hat or bonnet. One peculiarity in the description may serve for purposes of identification: part of the nail on the thumb on the left hand is deficient.

A clay pipe was also found beside the body and this was to coin the nickname, 'Clay Pipe Alice'. The pipe was confirmed to be hers by McCormack, who later said at the inquest that she 'smoked a great deal, and used a 'clay pipe'. Later that day, the body was identified and the same paper reported:

> Several hours elapsed before the woman was identified, but a man named John McCormack came forward during the day and recognised her as Alice McKenzie with whom he had lived for six or seven years, and who has for some time lodged with him as his wife at a common lodging house in Gun Street kept by a man named Tenpenny. McCormack stated that he

did not know whether the deceased had been married, and that the reason for her going out last night was that had a slight quarrel, and that she had never, to his knowledge, been out late at night previously. McCormack speaks of her as a hard-working woman and seems very much upset at the occurrence.

Now came some argument as to whether this was or was not a Ripper victim, or just a poor 'unfortunate' who had fallen victim to foul play by a disgruntled punter. Dr Phillips stated that the injuries did not suggest that the Ripper had struck again. James Monro, who had taken over as police commissioner from Sir Charles Warren, was to arrive at the scene a little after 3 am. It was later that day, however, that Monro reported to the Home Office that 'every effort will be made... to discover the murderer, who, I am inclined to believe, is identical with the notorious "Jack the Ripper" of last year'. Dr Thomas Bond, who was to examine Alice at the mortuary, gave the opinion that the injuries suffered were those of the Ripper. Robert Anderson, on holiday at the time of the murder, was later to state that the murder was not by the hand of the Ripper and that, 'the murder of Alice McKenzie was by another hand'. He also was to say that Monro had later changed his opinion and come to believe that her murder was 'an ordinary murder, and not the work of a sexual maniac'. With the actual Ripper murders occurring the previous autumn, and therefore still fresh in the minds of the public, one can only imagine the fears and anxiety that must have been running through their minds. The press, obviously latching on to the situation and no doubt fully exploiting the situation for financial gains, weren't going to let the murder slip, with the *East London Observer* reporting on 20 July 1889:

'The murder fiend is at his terribly ghastly work again. Countless pens are taken up again to write up the details of a mysterious and horrible crime in Whitechapel, and the heart of the nation is again harrowed by revolting stories of murder and mutilation. But what is there new to be said? Everything is on the same lines with the series of barbarous atrocities of last year – so nearly, indeed, does the crime tally with its ghastly predecessors that for all purposes we might as well tear out from the journals of that date a column or two describing one of the last years murders, after a name here and a street there, and the sad tale would be complete...'

The paper also said that Alice, 'Was the worse for drink, or one of the many outcasts who nightly frequent the alley to seek a shelter. On turning his (police constable Andrews) light down was horrified to find a woman lying on her back with a terrible gash in her throat'. The alley was also described for those unfamiliar with the location:

> The scene of the murder is probably one of the lowest quarters in the whole of East London, and a spot more suitable for the terror crime could hardly be found. On account of the evil reputation borne by this particular place, and the obscene of any inhabitants in the immediate vicinity. Castle-Alley, which is within a quarter of a mile of the scenes of the other murders, is principally composed of workshops, and is about 180 yards in length. The thoroughfare itself is blocked up, both day and night, with tradesmen's carts and wagons and costermonger's barrows, while on the opposite side to the workshops or store-houses is a high dead wall, above which, however, are the windows of some dwelling houses. This alley, which is entered by passage not more than a yard in width, between Nos. 124 and 125, Whitechapel – road, is entirely shut off from view of the main road, and would hardly be observed by the ordinary passer-by. At the end of the passage are the Broad school and Whitechapel wash-house, and the thoroughfare, from that end, leads into Newcastle and Wentworth streets, both of which are principally occupied by foreign Jews and the frequenters of common lodging houses. Although the houses in these two streets are densely populated, the people generally enter them from the Spitalfields end, especially at night time, on account of the dark and lonely nature of Castle-Alley, as well as the

evil reputation, it has always borne among the respectable portion of the inhabitants.

Alice McKenzie is doubted to be a victim of the Ripper by many and it certainly appears that this was a murder committed by another hand.

The Pinchin Street Torso

On Tuesday, 10 September 1889, the trunk of a female's body was discovered in one of the railway arches in Pinchin Street. The body was missing both legs and her head. James Monro attended the scene and was to send a seven page report to the Home Office and went on to say:

> This street is close to Berner Street which was the scene of one of the previous Whitechapel murders, it is not a very narrow street, but is lonely at night, and is patrolled every half hour by a constable on beat. The arch where the body was found abuts on the pavement. The constable discovered the body somewhat after 20 minutes past five on the morning of Tuesday (10 September). He is positive that when he passed the spot about five the body was not where it was found sometime between 5 and 5.30am... Although the body was placed in the arch on Tuesday morning the murder (and although there is not yet before me proof of the cause of death. I assume that there has been a murder) was not committed there nor then. There was almost no blood in the arch, and the state of the body itself showed that death took place about 36 hours or more previously. This then enables me to say that the woman was made away with probably on Sunday night, the 8th September this was dark on which one of the Whitechapel murder (Annie Chapman) was committed. Obviously this made the police believe that this was yet another victim of Jack the Ripper considering its date and close geographical

location to the accepted murders. Chief Inspector Donald Sutherland Swanson was quick to state that this murder had no similarities to those of Jack the Ripper saying... 'What becomes most apparent, is the absence of the attack upon the genitals as in the series of Whitechapel murders beginning at Buck's Row and ending in Miller's Court. Certainly if it were a murder there was time enough for the murderer to cut off the head and limbs there was time to mutilate as in the series mentioned.'

The press were quick to jump onto the murder and make their own presumptions. *The Herald*, in an article, went with the attention grabbing headline of 'A DIFFERENT METHOD OF MUTILATION' and would say, 'A perusal of the circumstances of former atrocities of this nature only serves to confuse the reader's mind as to the possible origin of this last crime. It differs from the Whitechapel series in the fact that the hands were left undisturbed, but it resembles them in the infliction of the deep longitudinal cut along the lower half of the truck...' Chief Commissioner James Monro, on 11 September 1889, quickly made his opinion on the comparison between the Pinchin Street torso and Jack the Ripper crimes: 'If this a fresh outrage by the Whitechapel murderer known by the horribly familiar nickname of Jack the Ripper... this murder committed in the murderers house would be a new departure from the system hitherto pursued by this ruffian. I am however inclined to believe that this case was not the work of the "Ripper".'

Was the Pinchin Street Torso a Murder Victim of the Ripper?

If she was a victim then the Ripper would have changed his modus operandi significantly. It's not unheard of for serial killers to do this of course so one has to be careful to dismiss this case out of hand readily but by taking a closer look we can conclude that this was highly unlikely to have been a victim of the Ripper. The Ripper victims had suffered evisceration whereas the Pinchin Street torso was subjected to mutilation. No body organs were removed in the Pinchin case, unlike the Ripper ones. Monro said, 'there is no removal of any portion of the organs of generation or intestines…' As for the location of the crime all the Ripper murders were carried out in the street except in one instance in Dorset Street (Mary Kelly) when, 'there were distinct traces of furious mania, the murderer having plenty of time at his disposal slashed and cut the body in all directions, evidently under the influence of frenzy'. When the murder of Kelly was mentioned as being committed inside, as the Pinchin Street torso murder must have been, Monro opined, 'probably in the lodging house of the murderer but… there is no sign of frenzied mutilation of the body, but of deliberate skillful dismemberment with a view to removal…' Monro concluded, 'These are all very striking departures from the practice of the Whitechapel murderer, and if the body had been found elsewhere in Whitechapel the supposition that death had been caused by the Ripper would probably not have been entertained…' The identity of the woman was never ascertained and the remains were buried on 5 October 1889 in the East London cemetery, Grange Park, Plaistow, Essex. She was buried in a case containing the body of a woman (unknown) found in Pinchin Street, St George-in-the-East, 10 September 1889. Today it is a widely accepted that the Pinchin Street torso murder was not one committed by the Ripper, and Monro, in his conclusion, summed up the reasoning perfectly.

Frances Coles

Frances Coles was murdered on 13 February 1891 and is the last to be named in the Whitechapel murder file. PC Ernest Thompson discovered her body at 2.15 am on Friday, 13 February 1891 as he was passing through an archway of the Great Eastern Railway between Swallow Gardens and Orman Street. His beat had taken him past the same spot at around 2.00 am and he was clear in stating that he had seen nothing untoward then. Upon him returning at 2.15 am, Thompson said he heard a man's footsteps walking away from him, and on looking into the arch, he observed a figure upon the ground. He then shone his light in the direction of the figure and discovered it to be a woman lying in a pool of blood, which was flowing from her throat area. He immediately blew his whistle for assistance and a neighbouring pair of beat officers, PC Hype and PC Hinton, quickly came running to his call. Also attending shortly afterwards was PC Elliot, who was, at the time, on plain clothes duty nearby in Royal Mint Street. PC Elliot would later say that it had all been very quiet until he heard the whistle of PC Thompson and that he'd not heard any cries from the victim. The officers began checking the woman for signs of life and felt a faint pulse. She was also quite warm to the touch. PC Hyde left the scene to fetch Dr Oxley, who, upon arriving at the scene, found the woman to be dead. PC Hinton was, at this time, sent to the police station to get a senior officer. Hinton returned with Inspector Flanagan who swiftly got the officers to search the immediate area and question anyone they thought to be suspicious. Flanagan ordered the body to remain in situ before he carried out a search of the close surroundings for clues and evidence. Police surgeon, Dr George Bagster Phillips, soon arrived and upon examining the body he quickly found two cuts to her throat that he said were 'sufficient to account for death'. He also opined that the position of the woman on the ground and the cuts did not tie this murder, 'with the series of murders which were accompanied by mutilations...' i.e. the Ripper murders. News spread fast and the following day *The Times* newspaper printed the following:

> Another murder, although not as fiendish as those which were enacted within a comparatively short period of one another in Whitechapel in 1888 and 1889, has been committed in the same district, and the many similar circumstances surrounding this latest mysterious crime seems to point to its being the work of the same person. The place, the time, the character of the victim, and other points of resemblance, recall in the most

obvious way the series of crimes associated in the popular mind with the so-called 'Jack the Ripper...'

The *East London Advertiser* dated the same day, Saturday, 14 February 1891, was not to go as far as *The Times* but instead conceded that this latest murder bore some similarities to the bona-fide Whitechapel murders. The deceased was yet to be identified as the inquest began on the 14 February and she was called by the coroner a 'woman unknown'. This quickly changed, however, as multiple people would view the body at the mortuary and before long the deceased was identified as Frances Coles. That same evening her father was found by DS Record and DS Kurhd. James William Coles resided in Bermondsey workhouse and Mary Ann Coles, the sister of the deceased who lived in Kingsland was also located and informed of the news. The *East London Advertiser* reported the following:

> The old man, who is very feeble, was taken to the mortuary in a cab, and had no difficulty in identifying the body as that of Frances Coles, his daughter. Another sister, named Selina, is also known to be living at Kingsland. The deceased was at one time engaged as a labeller at a wholesale chemists factory in the Minories. It has transpired that she left her lodgings in Thrawl Street about five weeks ago, but on Thursday last, between 9 and 10 o'clock, returned and asked her landlady, Mrs Hague, to let her come back, and promised to pay what she owed. She then went away, but Mrs Hague subsequently saw her in a public – house at the corner of Montague Street where she was with a man, who was treating her to a drink. He was of fair complexion and had a light moustache, Mrs Hague also identified the body...

With a description of a potential suspect to her murder, the police began a search for a murderer. It wasn't long before a name would be put to the limited description, that of James Thomas Sadler. Sadler had been drinking with Coles and was already known to her. He was a 53-year-old merchant seaman and fireman on the SS *Fez*, and had been a client of hers before they had drinks in the Princess Alice pub on 11 February. On the 12th they spent the day on a pub crawl that would leave them both much the worse for wear by the evening. Frances bought a black crepe hat at 25 Nottingham Street at approximately 7.30 pm, which cost 2s 6d, the money given to her by Sadler earlier. The man who served her was Peter Hawkes, who described her as 'three sheets in the wind'. Hawkes also noted Sadler (whom he later identified at a lineup at Leman Street Police Station) was peering through the window as Coles was in the shop. It later transpired that later that night, as Sadler and Coles were walking along Thrawl Street, Sadler was attacked by a woman wearing a red shawl who came at him from behind. With her were two men who then proceeded to rob Sadler of his watch and money. Coles allegedly just watched the altercation and didn't step in to help, which greatly angered Sadler. After the attack, they argued and both went their separate ways, he would later tell police at his interview. At 11.30 pm, a very intoxicated Coles turned up at her lodging house and sat at a bench in the kitchen. There she rested her head on her arms on the table and was quickly asleep. Sadler then turned up at the lodging house and quickly informed the night watchman, Charles Guiver, that he had been robbed. He also said he knew the robbers and had found them. Guiver then helped Sadler to clean up, at which point Guiver asked him to leave as he hadn't any money to pay for a bed that night. At 12.30 am on 13 February, Coles awoke and because she also had no money, she was likewise told to leave the house. A last sighting of Coles was made at 1.45 am when Coles met Ellen Calana, a fellow prostitute on Commercial Street. Calana later testified that she was solicited by 'a violent man in a cheese cutter hat'. She refused him and the man swiftly punched her in the face and gave her a black eye. He then approached Coles, who ignored the advice given by Calana, and headed off towards the Minories with him. At this point, Sadler had tried to get back on board his ship and had gotten involved in a violent fight with some dockworkers, which resulted in him receiving a head wound. Sadler then tried (twice) to gain entry to a lodging house in East Smithfield before then being spotted on the pavement outside the Royal Mint by Sergeant Edwards, who would later say Sadler appeared 'drunken and bloodied'. He questioned him about his injuries, to which Sadler said he'd been attacked by some men against the London Dock Gates that had also 'brutally ill-used him'. On the Saturday morning Sadler was tracked down and found in the Phoenix beer house where he was arrested with no resistance. He was then taken to Chief Inspector Donald Sutherland Swanson, who, after cautioning Sadler, questioned him in great and meticulous detail. Sadler admitted to knowing and being in the company of Coles but, of course, denied anything to do with her subsequent death. *The Times* would report on 17 February 1891:

> The police, after detaining the man James Thomas Sadler upwards of 40 hours in the Leman Street Police Station, considered that they had sufficient evidence to charge him with the wilful murder of the young woman who has now been positively identified as Frances Coles, and the charge was formally preferred by Detective Inspector Moore about 12 o'clock on Sunday night...

While following out their enquiries the police interestingly came upon a man named Donald Campbell who claimed that he had bought a knife from Sadler on the Friday morning for a shilling. Campbell had also said the knife's handle was in his words 'clammy' and the blade was stained. He then washed the knife and noticed the water was reddish in colour. Campbell then sold the knife but was able to provide the name of the person who'd sold it to him. As *The Times* would say, 'By that means it was secured. On Sunday morning Campbell went to the Leman Street Police Station and picked Sadler out from amongst a number of other men'.

With this, Sadler was eventually charged on 27 February with, 'wilfully causing the death of Frances Coles by cutting her throat with a knife on the 13th inst....'

The inquest came to a close on Friday, 27 February 1891, when Coroner Wynne Baxter was to tell the jury that there were 'many characteristics in common with the murders which had preceded it, but it was for the jury to decide, taking well into consideration Sadler's drunken condition, the conflicting evidence as to times and the connected account given by him of his movements before and after the murder was committed, whether they could fairly charge him with the dead, or must attribute it to some person or persons unknown...' Upon this the jury retired to consider their verdict only to return with the foreman to say 'We find that the deceased was wilfully murdered by some person or persons unknown, and we wish to say that we think the police did their duty in detaining Sadler'.

For a split second it appeared that the identity of Jack the Ripper was known and at last he had been caught and would serve the punishment befitting him, then all of a sudden, nothing... Sadler and his tale of being mugged was believed and although he admitted to being with Coles for a long period of time and then subsequently ending the night with an argument with her, the jury believed he'd played no part in the act of murder. His knife, it was later stated, was probably not sharp enough to inflict the cuts upon Coles' throat; this would be effectively the end of the case. Sadler was to appear before magistrates on Tuesday, 3 March 1891 where the prosecution were to tell the court:

> Having had the advantage of a consultation with the learned Attorney-General, who has carefully considered the evidence given in the course of the inquiry before the coroner, as well as the most able summing up to the jury impanelled before him, and having regard to the verdict returned by that jury. After a patient and exhaustive inquiry. I do not propose, on the materials at present in our possession, to proceed further with this prosecution, and sir, if it should meet with your approval, it will have the sanction both of the learned Attorney-General and of the Treasury authorities, that no further evidence should now be offended against the accused.

And with that Sadler was a free man and the murder of Frances Coles remained unsolved. Was this the Ripper at work again? In all probability not. As we saw, the area was a rough one, and encounters with the wrong people were commonplace. Frances Coles was most likely a victim of a 'punter' who hadn't paid and she threatened to inform on, or perhaps he was intoxicated and turned aggressive towards her, which led to her being killed. Whatever the case, we will never know the true identity of her murderer.

CHAPTER 11

Inside the Mind of the Ripper

On 25 October 1888, Sir Robert Anderson wrote to Dr Thomas Bond and asked him to examine the items accumulated thus far from the Ripper murders and asked him his opinion. Bond spent two weeks studying the case and replied back to Anderson on 10 November 1888, the day after Mary Jane Kelly had been killed (Dr Bond was to perform her autopsy). Bond's report said the following:

> I beg to report that I have read the notes of the 4 Whitechapel murders
>
> 1 Buck's Row
> 2 Hanbury Street
> 3 Berner Street
> 4 Mitre Square
>
> I have also made a post mortem examination of the mutilated remains of a woman found yesterday in a small room in Dorset Street:
>
> 1. All five murders were no doubt committed by the same hand. In the first four the throats appear to have been cut from left to right. In the last case owing to the extensive mutilation it is impossible to say in what direction the fatal cut was made, but arterial blood was found on the wall in splashes close to where the woman's head must have been lying.

2. All the circumstances surrounding the murders lead me to form the opinion that the woman must have been lying down when murdered and in every case the throat was first cut.

3. In the four murders of which I have seen the notes only, I cannot form a very definite opinion as to the time that had elapsed between the murder and the discovery of the body. In one case, that of Berner Street, the discovery appears to have been made immediately after the dead – in Buck's Row, Hanbury Street, and Mitre Square three or four hours could only have elapsed. In the Dorset Street case the body was lying on the bed at the time of my visit, 2 o'clock, quite naked and mutilated as in the annexed report – Rigor mortis had set in, but increased during the progress of the examination. From this it is difficult to say with any degree of certainty the exact time that had elapsed since death as the period varies from 6 to 12 hours before rigidity sets in. The body was comparatively cold at 2 o'clock and the remains of a recently taken meal were found in the stomach and scattered about over the intestines. It is, therefore, pretty certain that the woman must have been dead about 12 hours and the partly digested food would indicate; that death took place 3 or 4 hours after the food was taken, so one or two o'clock in the morning would be the probable time of the murder.

4. In all the cases there appears to be no evidence of struggling and the attacks were probably so sudden and made in such a position that the woman could neither resist or cry out. In the Dorset Street case the coroner found that the sheet to the right of the woman's head was very cut and saturated with blood, indicating that the face may have been covered with the sheet at the time of the attack.

5. In the four first cases the murderer must have attacked from the right side of the victim. In the Dorset Street case, he must have attacked from the front or from the left, as there would be no room for him between the wall and the part of the bed on which the woman was lying. Again, the blood had flowed down on the right side of the woman and spurted on to the wall.

6. The murderer would not necessarily be splashed or deluged with blood, but his hands and arm must have been covered and parts of his clothing must certainly have been smeared with blood.

7. The mutilations in each case excepting the Berner Street one were all of the same character and showed clearly that in all the murders the object was mutilation.

8. In each case mutilation was inflicted by a person who had no scientific nor anatomical knowledge. In my opinion he does not even possess the technical knowledge of a butcher or horse slaughterer or any person accustomed to cut up dead animals.

9. The instrument must have been a strong knife at least six inches long, very sharp, pointed at the top and about an inch in width. It may have been a clasp knife, a butcher knife or a surgeon's knife. I think it was no doubt a straight knife.

10. The murderer must have been of physical strength and of great coolness and daring. There is no evidence that he had an accomplice. He must in my opinion be a man subject to periodical attacks of homicidal and erotic mania. The character of the mutilations indicate that the man may

be in a condition sexually, that may be called satyriasis. It is of course possible that the homicidal impulse may have developed from a revengeful or brooding condition of the mind, or that Religious Mania may have been the original disease, but I do not think either hypothesis is likely. The murderer in external appearance is quite likely to be a quiet inoffensive looking man probably middle aged and neatly and respectably dressed. I think he must be in the habit of wearing a cloak or overcoat or he could hardly have escaped notice in the streets if the blood on his hands or clothes were visible.

11. Assuming the murderer to be such a person as I have just described he would probably be solitary and eccentric in his habits, also he is most likely to be a man without regular occupation, but with some small income or pension. He is possibly living amongst respectable persons who have some knowledge of his character and habits and who may have grounds for suspicion that he is not quite right in his mind at times. Such persons would probably be unwilling to communicate suspicions to the police for fear of trouble or notoriety, whereas if there were a prospect of reward it might overcome their scruples.

I am, Dear Sir,
Yours faithfully
Thos. Bond.

Although Jack the Ripper was not the world's first serial killer, Bond's profile of the Whitechapel murderer certainly was the first of its kind. Well over a century after the killings of 1888, the world-famous FBI even set out to profile the notorious murderer. They, of course, are well-versed in the behaviour of such murderers, given that the United States has had, and continues to have, a high rate of serial killers at any given time. We can establish firstly that the Ripper certainly didn't kill for financial gain, as his victims were all penniless and, except for Mary Jane Kelly. Sadism was not part of his profile either. The women were dispatched quickly by strangulation, which would render them unconscious and once upon the ground he would perform his mutilations of the body. According to profilers, this suggests a killer who wanted to dominate his victims using power and sexual violence. The violence used also shows a deep sense of hatred towards his victims, and the ultimate goal of the murders and mutilations was indicative of someone who wanted to erase the person completely. Given the time period, Jack the Ripper was a unique type of killer and the police of the day were most definitely not trained for the killings. A glance at the locations of the murders on a map suggests that the murderer lived in the general area of his victims, because he felt safe in the area and he could plan his attacks by knowing where the police would be and at what times their beats would take them past eventual crime scenes. He would also be able to plan his escape routes accordingly. Evidence for that comes in the piece of Catherine Eddowes' apron, which was dropped in Goulston Street. No doubt he was making his way home the night of the murder and dropped the article. It is mentioned that he may have had a respectable and charming manner about him as he approached his victims. Many people tend to view the character of Jack the Ripper as a tall man in a top hat and cloak, especially today, but this is most definitely not the case. An appearance like this would have meant he would have stuck out like the proverbial sore thumb and the opposite is far more likely to be the case. His clothing would have been that of the average East End man, meaning he could walk the streets without suspicion and also blend in with crowds easily.

Could the Ripper have been charming? Very possibly but not necessarily so. One must remember his victims. They were struggling women of the East End who were, mostly, desperate for their 'doss' money for the night. The very same thing occurred with the Ipswich Strangler, when Steve Wright was patrolling the red light district of Ipswich between October and December 2006 and five victims (at least) were taken by his hands. I remember watching the local news one evening and an interviewer asked a young girl, who had her back to the camera, if she would comment on the recent murders. She nervously replied that she was 'a bit wary about getting into cars' and when asked why she would continue, despite an unknown serial killer in the town, she replied, 'I need the money'. Steve Wright had killed four women at this point. The girl with her back to the camera being interviewed was Paula Clennell, a 24-year-old sex worker who, just a few days later, was to become Wright's fifth and final victim before his arrest on 18 December 2006. With this in mind, it's more than likely that the Ripper was simply an opportunist, using his victims' desperation to his advantage. Someone desperate to earn money for their shelter that evening might even approach the killer first, and, as she made contact with what she thought to be just another client, a switch would go off in his head. In a split second his hands would grasp onto her throat rendering her unable to scream for help. She would quickly become unconscious, literally in ten seconds, and wouldn't have had time to fight or struggle. Once on the ground, a swift cut to the throat, severing the main arteries, would result in death within a minute. He then would turn his attention to mutilations of the genital areas. He didn't have intercourse with the women, however, the attacks do strongly suggest sexual implications. Why would this be? Did he have a resentment for women so strong he had to remove their sexuality? This could indicate a woman in his history who subjected him to physical, mental or sexual abuse whilst growing up. Maybe his mother was herself a prostitute and his resentment came from seeing his mother struggle through life, often being beaten up and robbed, that triggered his deep hatred for women in the same position. One thing for sure is that the violence per murder escalated significantly. Was his urge to mutilate finally realised with Mary Jane Kelly? Was she his magnum opus, so to speak? Mary Jane Kelly definitely saw a level of manic barbarity that took at least two hours to complete. The privacy of an indoor setting no doubt was the Ripper's dream scenario where he could completely destroy the young girl to the point where even those few close to her would not recognise her. FBI profilers, John Douglas and Roy Hazelwood, came up with 10 characteristics of Jack the Ripper in 1988, which are as follows:

1. The Ripper would be a white male.
2. Between 25 and 35 years old.
3. Lived locally to the Whitechapel/Spitalfields area.
4. A loner, who was more likely unmarried.
5. As a child he would have had an absent father and a dominant mother figure.
6. A mental or physical disability or deformity, which made him feel different from others.
7. A solitary job, which kept him away from social encounters.
8. Seen as quiet and timid to those who knew him, he would be perceived as a little odd.
9. Beneath the surface would lie a deep and resentful aggression, which would explode during bouts of low self-esteem.
10. He would not feel guilt or remorse for his crimes, and in a way considered them justified.

Special Agent Douglas would further add:

We would look for someone below or above average in height and/or weight. May have problems with speech, a scarred complexion, physical illness, or injury. We would not expect this type of offender to be married. If he was married in the past it would have been to someone older than himself and the marriage would have been for a short duration. He is not adept in meeting people socially and the major extent of his heterosexual relationships would be with prostitutes. The offender does not look out of the ordinary. However, the clothing he wears at the time of the assaults is not his everyday dress. He wants to project to unsuspecting female prostitutes that he has money. He comes from a family where he was raised by a domineering mother and a weak, passive father. In all likelihood, his mother drank heavily and enjoyed the company of many men. As a result, he failed to receive consistent care and contact with stable adult role models. This could have resulted in the would-be serial killer having an introverted nature, lashing out violently as a result of his frustration. As well as being an introvert, the killer would likely be regarded as a shy and retiring loner who would also take great care over his appearance. He drinks in the local pub and after a few spirits, he becomes more relaxed and finds it easier to engage in conversation. After he leaves the pub, he would stroll throughout the Whitechapel neighbourhood with lower inhibitions. He lives or works in the Whitechapel area. After each killing, he would return to a safe area where he could wash the blood from his hands and get rid of soiled clothing. So the next question and probably most important after who was JTR is why did he stop? It is not unheard of for serial killers to stop suddenly and even take up killing again many years later. Several reasons could exist as to why he stopped when he did.

1. He was almost caught.
2. He was actually caught and imprisoned on another unrelated crime.
3. He committed suicide or died of illness/natural causes.
4. He was found out by close friends/relatives.
5. He was committed to an asylum.

He may very well have been almost caught as the police hugely ramped up their efforts after Mary Jane Kelly's death, with all premises in the immediate area being searched and landlords questioned, and over 500 informants were told to keep their eyes open on every corner. We must assume from the profiling that he was a local resident of the area and now, with the community watching, he may very well have stopped through fear of capture and the punishment he'd have been handed down i.e., death by hanging. It's also possible that he was caught for a totally unrelated crime. He may have been arrested for theft or an assault on a person. He may also have died. There was a flu pandemic in 1887 and, given the poverty and unsanitary conditions of London in Victorian times, the Ripper may have fallen foul to illness or malnutrition. This, of course, assumes the Ripper was of the same social class as the women he killed. He may have been mentally ill to the point he took his own life after the killing of Kelly. Perhaps he had a change of conscience, and being filled with regret and remorse for his crimes, he then killed himself. This is a long shot, of course, but nothing is out of the question. He may have been discovered by friends and family – perhaps after the Kelly incident he went home drenched in blood and they confronted him and committed him to an asylum. Jack the Ripper certainly wasn't the first serial killer in the world but he definitely became the godfather of serial killers and with his reign of terror, policing policies and protocols had to change and change quickly.

CHAPTER 12

The Identity of the Ripper Revealed

We have studied the case, examined the evidence and looked at the candidates for the Ripper, but one suspect has been omitted until now and, I believe, the man responsible for the Ripper murders has been hiding in plain sight all along.

We met this man before, very early on in the case, and he goes by the name of Charles Allen Lechmere. Casting our minds back to when we first met Lechmere, or Cross as he called himself at the time, at the scene of the very first murder, that of Mary Ann Nichols on Friday, 31 August 1888 in Buck's Row. He was the man who, upon his usual early morning walk to work, came across what he suspected to be a tarpaulin in the road, which, upon closer inspection, turned out to be the body of what would become the first of the five canonical Jack the Ripper victims. With so many suspects put forward in the Whitechapel mystery it is often a case of falling at the first fence because they simply cannot be placed at the scene of any murder. But straight away, Lechmere can be, and was. That being said, of course, Lechmere cannot be accused of the crimes on this basis alone, he may have been simply in the wrong place at the wrong time, but looking deeper, one can soon begin to piece the puzzle together, and the evidence very quickly begins to mount up. Some may say it's coincidental but as the old adage goes, 'once is chance, twice is coincidence, third time's a pattern'. So, before we plunge into his full involvement in the case, let's meet the man himself.

Charles Allen Lechmere was born on 5 October 1849 in Soho, the son of John Allen Lechmere and Maria Louisa Lechmere (née Roulson).

When Charles was very young his father, a bootmaker by trade, left the family home, along with his wife and his four children, to begin a new life and eventually a new family in Northampton. In 1858, Maria, who by then was living with her children in Whitechapel, married a police constable named Thomas Cross who was 9 years her junior and was 23 at the time. The problem with this marriage was that it was a bigamous one; Maria and John had not yet legally separated, the judicial punishment in Victorian England for this crime if you were a woman was to either be acquitted or a sentence of less than seven days in prison, but most cases were acquitted. In 1859, Charles and his sister, Emily, were baptised 'Lechmere' and the family next appear on the census of 1861, where all four members of the household were given the surname of Cross. The reason for this is unclear, given the children were previously baptised Lechmere, but it is very likely that the census form was filled in by Thomas Cross. On the same form, the family address was given as Thomas Street, this was later to be named Pinchin Street, a location we have previously mentioned if you remember? By the time of the next census, that of 1871, Charles was living at Mary Ann Street and had left the Cross family home. He was now 21 years old and had married Elizabeth Bostock, also 21 years old. They had married the year prior in Christchurch, Spitalfields. Sadly for Charles, the year before his marriage, his sister Emily was to pass away in the summer, due to phthisis exhaustion – today known as tuberculosis – aged just 22. Ten years later, the 1881 census sees the Lechmere family now in residence at James Street, with Charles and Elizabeth having four children aged between 1 and 7. The total number of children they would parent would eventually rise to eleven. The census of 1891 shows the family living at 22 Doveton Street, and this is right in the heart of Ripper country and a place the family had moved to in June of 1888. While Charles was busy at this time, his mother was also far from idle. Thomas Cross, her husband in the bigamous marriage, had died in 1869 and Maria had wasted little time in marrying a shoemaker named Joseph Forsdike in 1872. Forsdike was ten years her senior but, again, this marriage was bigamous. Charles' father, John, wasn't to pass away until 1879. The 1881 census is interesting in that it tells us that a 6-year-old girl named Mary Jane Lechmere lived in Pinchin Street with Maria and Joseph. This child was Charles' daughter and the reason why she was living there is unclear but we know that on the 1891 census she was still listed as living with her grandmother, albeit at George Street in St George. Joseph had died in 1889 in hospital and Maria had changed occupations. In 1881 she was listed as a dressmaker, but in 1891 she had become a horseflesh dealer. Mary Jane was to stay with her grandmother and would eventually marry Harry Alfred Goodson in 1899 when she was aged 26. By this time Maria was 74 years old and was a corn chandler (a person selling grain products). She was to live to see the twentieth century, dying in late 1901 aged 76. During this period, Charles was moving around himself. In 1901 he was still in Doveton Street but not in his previous abode of number 22, but next door at number 24. In 1902 he moved to 24 Carlton Road, where he was owner of a grocer and sweet stuff shop listed at the same address. Lechmere was to die two days before Christmas on 23 December 1920 of a brain haemorrhage, leaving his wife a total of £262, which in today's money (2024), equates to approximately £14,676. Elizabeth was to live until just after the outbreak of the Second World War, dying in 1940. The couple were buried within the same cemetery of Tower Hamlets, but not in the same grave, Charles was laid to rest in a common unmasked grave, whereas Elizabeth had a marked grave at the opposite end of the cemetery to Charles.

CHAPTER 13

Completing the Puzzle

We have looked at a very brief biography of Charles Allen Lechmere and now we must become amateur sleuths to connect all the pieces of the puzzle, and install Lechmere at the top of the suspect list.

We begin with the first victim, Mary Ann Nichols, on Friday, 31 August 1888 at 3.15 am. Setting the scene, we know the temperature was a cool 8°c, it was dry and the sky was partly cloud covered, a thin waning crescent moon was casting a small, feeble amount of light onto the streets of Whitechapel. The sun was below the horizon and twilight would begin at 3.50 am, with sunrise occurring at 5.20 am. At 3.15 am, PC John Neil (officer no 97) of J Division, Bethnal Green, entered Buck's Row from a westerly direction and headed towards Brady Street upon his regular beat. He would later state that he 'saw no one then', also saying he was, 'never far away from the spot'. He did encounter two men employed at the slaughterhouse on Winthrop Street as he passed through Whitechapel Road and passed up Buck's Row.

3.30 am–3.45 am

Charles Allen Cross (Lechmere) claimed to have left his home at 22 Doveton Street, Bethnal Green at 3.30 am to go to work at Messrs Pickford & Co. on Broad Street, where he was employed as a 'carman', today the equivalent to a 'white van man'. He would later confess to being 'behind time' when he left for work. It should be noted that

Buck's Row was under half a mile from his home, around 7 minutes' walk. As Lechmere turned into Buck's Row he spotted an object in the distance that he initially believed to be a tarpaulin. He approached it only to discover that the tarpaulin was, in fact, the body of Mary Ann Nichols. The estimated time now was 3.37 am. He remained with the body until he was joined by Robert Paul who himself was going to work. Paul arrived at the scene at 3.45 am. By this time, Cross had been with the body for eight minutes. This appears odd, given that he was 'behind time'. Surely, upon discovering the body he would have gone for help after, say, a minute or two after finding her? Nevertheless, Robert Paul and Cross examined the body and then both men agreed to tell the first policeman that they encountered. Cross later said at that time there was 'nobody there when he and the other man (Paul) left'. Paul himself would say also he saw nobody running away and that he'd spent five minutes in Buck's Row, from encountering Cross until they left for a policeman. The two men would find PC Jonas Mizen first, on Hanbury Street. At 3.45 am, PC John Neil came back into Buck's Row from the westerly direction of Thomas Street or Baker's Row. A look at the time tells us that he could only have just missed Cross and Paul as they themselves left the scene. From this, we can deduce a time discrepancy of around five minutes. This being said, the times given by Cross must be wrong, and he was likely on the scene earlier than he initially thought, perhaps as early as 3.17 am, two minutes after PC John Neil had left the area for the first time around at 3.15 am. Upon PC Neil entering Buck's Row the second time, he discovered the body of Nichols in an empty street. Turning his bullseye lamp towards the body, he saw blood oozing from a deep wound in her throat. He noted the woman was 'quite warm from the joints upwards'. He scanned the scene but did not see any indication of wheel tracts, which indicated that she had not been dropped off at the scene after being killed elsewhere. Upon speaking with the two horse slaughterers he'd met earlier, they said they 'knew nothing of the affair, and had not heard any screams'. Remember, the body was quite warm and the early morning was just 8°c, and this indicates that she had not been deceased long. After the heart stops beating, the body begins to chill in a phase known as algor mortis. On average, a drop of 1°c occurs per hour after death, so some could say that she could have died earlier, but PC John Neil would be well aware of his timings because of his beat. Dr Henry Llewellyn arrived at the scene at about 4.00 am and would later testify that Nichols had not been dead more than half an hour after his arrival. The time of death is thus 3.30 am at the latest. He also added that death would have been instantaneous, and the abdominal injuries would have taken under five minutes to perform and were made post mortem. The next we hear of Cross and Paul is at the inquest, on day two to be exact, on Monday, 3 September 1888. A man going by the name of 'Chas Allen Cross [Lechmere]' gave evidence and repeated the events written above; Cross had given the authorities a false name. We remember from earlier that Cross was his stepfather's name and he only appears with this name on a census, but at all other times he used Lechmere. So why falsify his name at an inquest? It is unclear why, but this is also suspicious. I mean, what criminal, no matter the offence, gives out their real name? Food for thought as we continue. The previous day, the *Lloyd's Weekly* issued a special edition of their paper and carried a witness account given by Robert Paul, 'It was exactly a quarter to four when I passed up Buck's Row to my work as a carman for a Covent Garden market. It was dark, and I was hurrying along, when I saw a man standing where the woman was.'

On the first day of the inquest on 1 September, PC John Neil gave testimony that he'd come across the deceased at 3.45 am in Buck's Row. He reiterated that there was nobody about and that he'd patrolled that very spot some thirty minutes earlier and that nobody was in situ at 3.15 am either. Neither Cross nor Paul are mentioned. PC Jonas Mizen isn't mentioned. It would appear to a juror that Neil was first on scene. He then went on to describe Nichols' body, with blood oozing from her throat, lying on her back and with her clothes in disarray. This day also had testimony from Dr Henry Llewellyn, who stated his arrival on scene at 4.00 am and that Nichols had sustained severe injuries to her throat and that no sign of a struggle had taken place. He put her time of death as 3.30 am.

The Daily News was to report the testimony of Cross as follows, 'Charles A. Cross Carman, said he had been in the employment of Messrs Pickford and co for some years'. The report continued,

> On Friday morning, he left home about half past three to go to work, and passing through Buck's Row he saw on the opposite side something lying against a gateway. In the dark he could not tell at first what it was. It looked like a tarpaulin sheet, but walking to the middle of the road he saw it was the figure of a woman.
>
> At the same time he heard a man about forty yards away coming up Buck's Row in the direction the witness had himself come. He stepped back and waited for the newcomer, who started on one side, as if he feared that the witness meant to knock him down. The witness said, 'come and look over here. There's a woman'.
>
> They both went across to the body, and the witness took hold of the hands while the other man stopped over her head to look at her. The hands were cold and limp, and the witness said, 'I believe she's dead'. Then he touched her face, which felt warm. The other man placed his hand on her heart, saying, 'I think she's breathing, but it's very little if she is'. He suggested that they should 'shift her', meaning in the witness's opinion that they should seat her upright. The witness replied. 'I am not going to touch her'. The woman's legs were uncovered. Her bonnet was off, but close to her head.
>
> The witness did not notice that her throat was cut, as the night was very dark.

He and the other man left the deceased, and in Baker's Row they saw PC Mizen whom they told that a woman was lying in Buck's Row. The witness added, 'She looks to me either dead or drunk', and the other man remarked, 'I think she's dead'. The policeman answered, 'All right'. The other man left the witness soon afterwards. He appeared to be a carman, but the witness had never seen him before. At the time of his encounter with Cross and Paul, PC Mizen was located at the junction of Hanbury Street and Baker's Row in the duty of 'knocking up', a service performed by policeman on their early morning beats to wake local residents so they would be able to get to work on time a sort of Victorian alarm clock if you will. PC Mizen later testified that Cross said to him, 'You are wanted down there' while pointing in the direction of Buck's Row, as reported by some newspaper reports, but other newspaper quoted PC Mizen as saying that Cross said, 'You are wanted in Buck's Row by a policeman, a woman is lying there'. There is a clear discrepancy in these statements, with both being reported to have been said by PC Mizen. We must remember that we are looking in with hindsight and lots of different accounts to study, but at the time this was happening in real time so one has to step back and think in that moment, not the one we are currently in. Did Mizen assume he was wanted in Buck's Row because he came upon PC Neil at the scene and believed Cross and Paul had been sent by him or did Cross actually say there was a policeman needing assistance there? Did reporters make a mistake? Did Cross say 'you're wanted down there', meaning it in broader terms, as in, you (being an officer of the law, a crime has been committed) are wanted down there? At the inquest Cross, when asked, 'did you tell constable Mizen that another policeman wanted him in Buck's Row?' replied 'No, because I did not see a policeman in Buck's Row'. So, in conclusion to this first murder, we know that Cross arrived in Buck's Row alone and that he spent at least eight minutes with the body of Nichols before Robert Paul arrived. We also know that Cross and Paul found PC Mizen and that Cross alerted Mizen to an incident in Buck's Row and gave a false name at the inquest: Cross, instead of Lechmere. At the inquest PC Mizen is supposed to have said that Cross asked him to go to Buck's Row to assist a fellow constable, yet Cross had said no policeman was there and it was pure coincidence that PC Neil was on scene when PC Mizen entered Buck's Row. We must question not only the eight minutes Cross was with the body alone, but also his reluctance to touch the body in any way once Paul arrived. Paul lowered her skirt to cover her decency but neither man could see the deep wound upon her throat as it was covered up. Her abdomen was cut open from sternum to groin, but again these wounds were covered and went unseen by both men. The fact these wounds were covered up would strongly suggest that the killer had done so upon being disturbed. It all goes back to 'fight or flight'. If you run you are suspect. Paul would obviously have called out for help as the killer fled and it wouldn't have been long before an officer caught him, but if you stay at the scene and act as surprised as the next man you instantly become only a witness to the discovery of a dead body. All the makings of an extremely calm, calculating killer.

What about blood? Both Cross and Paul made no mention of blood but blood was evident when PC Neil arrived, and PC Mizen noted that, upon his arrival, blood was draining from the body and into the gutter. This highly suggests that Nichols 'bled out' after Cross and Paul left to find a policeman, implying that Nichols had literally been killed only a couple of minutes before Paul encountered Cross at the scene. Time wise, there was no blood around the body at 3.45 am to a substantial amount being present upon PC Mizen's arrival at 4.20 am, after completing his beat and knocking up duties. From the deep wounds on the neck and abdomen, the blood would have simply oozed out with no time to coagulate due to the severity of the injuries. There would have been no blood spurting if she was strangled before the throat was cut as the heart would not have been pumping the blood, giving further cause to the oozing out theory. Time is of great importance too. If Cross did leave his home in Doveton Street at 3.30 am, the seven-minute journey would mean he arrived at 3.37 am. He said he was 'behind time', so why did he stay so long at the scene if he was already late? There can be only one explanation: he was the killer and wasn't 'behind time' at all. He had left home at his usual time to arrive in Buck's Row, where he met and killed Nichols. The false name is also of interest, why give the name Cross instead of Lechmere? He gave his correct address and place of work so why not the correct name? He even appeared at the inquest, so although he appears to have nothing to hide, he still hid his name. Was he a cold-blooded killer who was wary of being caught by the police or was it something done in a momentary lapse of panic? We will never know, but it is definitely something that should have been picked up at the inquest.

Annie Chapman
(Body discovered 6.00 am, 8 September 1888)

It makes sense that a serial killer operates within the safety of their own location. To be in this environment is vital to their success because they know every road like the back of their hands. They can work out how to find a victim in a secluded place, the police routes and times of the area. All they have to figure out is a method of despatch. As previously discussed, Annie Chapman was discovered on the morning of Saturday, 8 September 1888 at 6.00 am in the background of 29 Hanbury Street. Her clothes were lifted over her body with her legs drawn up, her feet upon the ground and knees turned outwards. Her uterus had been moved, along with the upper part of her vagina, and two-thirds of her bladder. Her abdomen had been ripped open and her intestines were severed from the mesenteric attachments and placed upon her right shoulder. Her face was swollen and her tongue, also swollen, protruded between her front teeth. The neck cut twice down to the very bone. The barbarity of the murder had certainly ramped up and this may very well have been born out of frustration, as the attack on Mary Ann Nichols was prematurely interrupted, and the killer's bloodlust stopped in its tracks. No witness was at the scene to this murder but it is indicated that Chapman died at around 5.30 am. The doctor on scene, Dr George Bagster Phillips, upon examining her, said she'd been dead for at least two hours before his arrival and possibly longer. His examination took place at 6.30 am, which would indicate a time of death of 4.30 am, but if we could stretch the timing back another forty-five minutes to 3.45 am, this could easily be when Lechmere was making his way to work, as in the case of Mary Ann Nichols. Lechmere's route to work, using the shortest distance, would take him down – you guessed it – Hanbury Street. Circumstantial evidence, but nonetheless the location and times can be easily made to fit.

The Double Event

Elizabeth Stride (Body discovered 1.00 am, Sunday, 30 September 1888)
Catherine Eddowes (Body discovered 1.45 am, Sunday, 30 September 1888)

We've covered these murders previously, but one question even asked today is, was Elizabeth Stride an actual victim of the Ripper?

Stride was murdered between 12.50 and 12.55 am on 30 September in Dutfield's Yard, Berner Street, Whitechapel. Louis Diemschutz was driving his horse and cart into the yard when his horse shied away and, looking down, saw the body of the dead woman. Stride had her throat cut but there were no further mutilations upon her body. Had the killer been interrupted by Diemschutz and so had to flee the scene with his work unfinished? The killing was instantly attributed to the Ripper by the police because the coroner, Wynne Baxter, had said that the murder of Stride was performed by the same person that had killed Mary Ann Nichols and Annie Chapman. It must be also noted that prominent figures in the case, Abberline, Anderson, Macnaghten, Smith and Swanson concluded also that she was a victim of the Ripper. But one must wonder the outcome of the scenario of the attack had Catherine Eddowes not been killed three-quarters of an hour later. Dr Phillips was, however, not convinced that Stride was a true Ripper victim. Stride had not been strangled before her death unlike Chapman. And of greater interest is the fact that the knife used to kill Tabram, Nichols, Chapman, Eddowes and Kelly was a long one, whereas the knife used to kill Stride had been a short, round one. One could suggest the Ripper had changed his MO, but that said, why then kill again within the hour with the long knife before going on to kill Mary Jane Kelly with a long knife too? An even more daring piece of evidence is that the killer of Elizabeth Stride was right handed whereas the other victims were slain and butchered by a left-handed killer. Dr Phillips himself noted that Stride was lying flat on her back when her throat was slit from her left carotid artery, across her windpipe, and stopping just to the right of her Adam's apple. He then said that the killer would've been to the left of her body whilst performing the cut, and thus away from any blood flowing from the wound. It must be noted too that a small skin abrasion measuring 1.5 inches wide was on Stride's right jaw. One could assume that was the impression of a thumbprint from the killer's left hand as he placed his hand over her mouth, whilst cutting her throat with the knife in his right hand. Performing this action means the knife being drawn from left to right. This clearly demonstrates that the attacker was right handed but indications strongly suggest the Ripper was left handed. Now, an interesting thought is that perhaps the Ripper was ambidextrous. This may have been the case but people with this ability still normally favour their stronger hand over the other. The wound was clearly executed, indicating that the stronger hand was used. Again, this highly favours a right-handed killer. The locality of the attack and murder are also very different compared to the other four locations. The lighting conditions were completely different, for example, if you include Martha Tabram, Mary Ann Nichols, Annie Chapman, Catherine Eddowes and Mary Jane Kelly, they were all killed in poorly illuminated areas, whereas Stride was killed in a well-lit area near to a club. Why would the Ripper choose such a location when the others were so poorly lit? Surely, he was opening himself up to being captured, especially at such an early time (12.50–12.55 am) and next to a club. Either the Ripper was getting over confident or it was the work of another. If not the Ripper, can we find a likely culprit? The first logical subject would be her partner, Michael Kidney. In modern day crimes like this, the first port of call is the deceased partner. PC William Smith and Israel Schwartz had both seen Stride on the night before her death. PC Smith would remark that the man he saw with her was acting like her lover. However, the man described by Schwartz was not the same man as seen by Smith, and yet this man must have been her killer, given the description of the scene at that time. As we remember, Schwartz ran in panic and didn't intervene. Could the man Schwartz saw have been Michael Kidney? We know that Kidney was certainly possessive of Stride, as he would padlock her in their room and had even told the police that had expected to find her locked in the room when he came home. Little did he know that Stride was in possession of a key and thus was able to free herself. The possibility is that Kidney came home and found her gone before going out to find her. He may have seen her with this other man and become enraged, and after confronting her, killed her in a fit of rage, a case of, if I can't have you nobody can. At the inquest he gave details and some interesting exchanges occurred as reported in *Lloyd's Weekly* newspaper dated Sunday, 7 October 1888:

> Michael Kidney called, and examined... I live at 38, Dorset Street, Spitalfields. I am a waterside labourer.
>
> **Coroner:** Have you seen the body in the mortuary?
>
> **Kidney:** Yes
>
> **Coroner:** Do you know what her name was?
>
> **Kidney:** Elizabeth Stride
>
> **Coroner:** How long have you known her?
>
> **Kidney:** About three years
>
> **Coroner:** How long has she been living with you?
>
> **Kidney:** Nearly all the time
>
> **Coroner:** Do you know what her age was?
>
> **Kidney:** Between 36 and 38. She told me she was 35. She told me that she was a Swede, and that she was born three miles from Stockholm. She said she first came to England to see it, but I have great doubts about this. She afterwards told me that she came to England with a family in a situation. She told me that she was a widow, and that her husband was a ship's carpenter belonging to Sheerness.
>
> **Coroner:** Did he ever keep a coffee-house?

Completing the Puzzle

Kidney: She told me he did at Chrisp-Street, Poplar, and that he was drowned in the *Princess Alice* disaster

Coroner: Was the roof of her mouth deficient?

Kidney: Yes

Coroner: When did you last she deceased alive?

Kidney: On Tuesday week. I left her on friendly terms in Commercial Street as I was coming from work between nine and ten o'clock at night. I got home half an hour afterwards, and she had been in and gone out. I did not see her again until I saw the body at the mortuary. She left me through drink. She had done it before and came back. I treated her the same as I would a wife.

Things then became a little strange…

Inspector Reid: Were you intoxicated?

Kidney: Yes

Coroner: What information have you?

Kidney: I have heard something said which would lead me to get a good deal more information if I had police help

Jury member: You must have special information to have wanted a detective?

Kidney: I had

Coroner: Well, give us your information, we are all interested in catching the murderer?

Kidney: I believe I could capture him if I had control of the force. If I could place 100 men, the murderer would be caught in the act.

Inspector Reid: But you have no information to give?

Kidney: If I placed the men, one of them would catch him in the act.

So, as we can see, there is a very high chance that Elizabeth Stride was not a victim of Jack the Ripper at all and it may be mere coincidence that Stride died on the same night as an actual bona-fide Ripper murder. Regarding Charles Lechmere, all we can say is the location of Stride's murder, Berner Street, is out of the way of Lechmere's walk to work from Doveton Street to Broad Street. But a small light at the end of the tunnel for those that remain staunch in their belief this was a Ripper killing argue that Lechmere's mother lived close by in Cable Street and that Lechmere may have killed Stride either coming from or going to her residence. If you believe in this theory then Elizabeth Stride was a victim of Charles Lechmere, and thus a Ripper victim. If not (as this author does not) then Elizabeth Stride was the victim of an altercation totally unrelated to the Whitechapel Ripper murders.

Catherine Eddowes

If the murder of Elizabeth Stride is highly in doubt then the murder of Catherine Eddowes is certainly a Ripper killing. To recap on the circumstances leading up to her death: at 8.00 pm on the night of Saturday, 29 September 1888, City PC Louis Robinson, whilst on patrol, encountered Eddowes as she was surrounded by a crowd outside of 29 Aldgate High Street. Eddowes was highly intoxicated and lying in a slumped leap on the pavement. PC Robinson, with the help of PC George Simmons, took her to Bishopsgate Police Station. At 8.45 pm, Sergeant James Byfield documents Eddowes' arrival at the station. At 8.50 pm, PC Robinson looked into her cell to see her fast asleep, smelling of drink. At 9.45 pm, City of London PC George Hutt took over the prisoners and visited the occupied cells every half an hour during the course of the night.

At 12.15 am, Sunday, 30 September, Eddowes had awoken and was heard softly singing to herself in her cell. At 12.30 am, she shouted out, asking when she would be released. 'When you are capable of taking care of yourself', came the reply from PC Hutt. 'I can do that now', Eddowes responded. At 12.55 am, Sergeant Byfield asked PC Hutt to see if any prisoners were capable of being released and Eddowes was found to be sober. At this point, she gave her name as Mary Ann Kelly, residing at 6 Fashion Street. She was then released.

At 1.00 am, she left the station, asking PC Hutt, 'What time is it?' 'Too late for you to get anything to drink' Hutt replied, she then stated, 'I shall get a damn fine hiding when I get home'. To which an unsympathetic Hutt retorted, 'And serve you right, you had no right to get drunk'. Pushing the door open, he said, 'This way misses ... Please pull it to'. 'All right', she replied and ended by saying 'Goodnight, old cock'.

This is when she made a fatal mistake. As she came out of the doorway, she turned left, which took her the opposite way to the direction she needed to get home to Flower and Dean Street. The direction she fatefully took was leading back towards Aldgate High Street where she'd been found earlier, drunk. This journey would have taken her down Houndsditch, passing the entrance to Duke Street, which led to Church Passage and into Mitre Square.

At 1.35 am, Eddowes was seen talking with a man at the corner of Duke Street and Church Passage by Joseph Hyam Levy and Harry Harris. Lawende said the man was about 30 years old, 5 foot 7 inches tall, with a fair complexion, a moustache and a medium build. He was wearing a pepper and salt-coloured jacket, loosely fitting, a grey cloth cap with a peak, a reddish handkerchief around his neck. Lawende identified the clothes worn by Eddowes after seeing her at the mortuary.

At 1.45 am, PC Edward Watkins found the body of Eddowes in Mitre Square.

Between 1.35 and 1.45 am, Eddowes sustained savage injuries. Her throat was cut and her abdomen was exposed, her intestines were drawn out and placed over her right shoulder, extensive injuries were also on her face, she had also had her left kidney removed. In just ten minutes she had gone from alive to absolutely eviscerated, her killer worked quick and fast and there is absolutely no doubt the man seen talking to her was Jack the Ripper, there would certainly have been no time for her to meet a different man and to be killed. Again, the Ripper had been seen by witnesses and again had evaded capture.

What can we determine from this murder and can we place Lechmere there? Again, everything is circumstantial, but we can say straight off the bat that the description given of the man talking to Eddowes certainly matches Lechmere in all aspects, but this is not enough to call him the Ripper on this alone (though it is a great start). Let us begin with the time and location. This murder was obviously earlier than the previous ones, and this can easily be explained by the fact it took place on a Saturday night; in the Victorian era, Sunday was a day of rest, as the working week was Monday to Saturday, and this allows for him to be available at the time. The location of her murder followed a path to Lechmere's route to work that he had walked for twenty years, he literally knew these streets like the back of his hand. This is coupled with the fact that Lechmere's mother lived at Mary Ann Street at the time which he would have obviously known well and is on his way home back to Doveton Street. We must also remember that this is the location where a piece of Eddowes' apron was taken from the body before subsequently dropped by the killer in the doorway of 108–119 Wentworth Model Buildings in Goulston Street. Again, this is directly between Mitre Square and Doveton Street. This all again is circumstantial but surely this is all more than coincidence? What about the graffiti on the wall above the piece of apron? Was this the writing of the Ripper? This we will never know as it was washed away, due to this murder being committed within the City of London and thus it was ultimately their decision to remove it due to the fear of racial incitement against the Jewish population living within the area.

Mary Jane Kelly (Body discovered 9 November 1888)

Mary Jane Kelly was the youngest of the Ripper victims, and also unique in that she had been killed and literally butchered inside of a building. One thing that strikes us instantly is the length of time from the last victim(s) is this one, some forty days almost six full weeks had elapsed and without a shadow of doubt the population of Whitechapel must have begun to feel at ease, albeit, tentatively, but the calm was certainly to be followed by the storm.

Another question must be, why was this murder committed so long after the previous events? Again, the frustrating answer must be, we will never fully know for sure but we can throw out some ideas as to why the Ripper went on a short hiatus:

1. He was away from the area due to work/family commitments.
2. He got ill.
3. He had injured himself at the scene of the Eddowes murder (hence taking a piece of the apron to cover a wound?)

It is highly likely that the true reason was either option 2 or 3, but one thing we do know is that when he returned, he returned with a vengeance. Of all the Whitechapel murders, that of Mary Jane Kelly is by far the most interesting from a criminologist perspective. The level of brutality reached a level never before seen and was never to be surpassed. As mentioned before, the uniqueness of this murder was its indoors setting. A question I have often asked myself is, did the Ripper and Kelly know each other prior to that fateful night? All the other victims were living amongst other people at the time of their deaths, but Kelly was living alone after Joseph Barnett left Miller's Court on 30 October following a quarrel. Could it have been that the Ripper knew this in advance and knew that, once in the confinement of her room, he would be undisturbed and be able to perform the deeds that he had ultimately dreamt of. This scenario is a possibility and the Ripper could very well have hand-picked his victim. With Kelly, it appears that she had undressed prior to her murder, a sure sign she was comfortable within the presence of this man. Was it because he was calm and trustworthy, or did she know him? Could he have used her services before? All of this is subject to conjecture, of course, but certainly food for thought for the reader. Regarding the location of her death in Miller's Court, it is geographically close to Annie Chapman's murder in Hanbury Street, and well within the vicinity of Charles Lechmere and his regular route through Whitechapel. He virtually walked past Miller's Court whilst on his way to work and she would have solicited on Commercial Street, which he had to cross, so he could very well have met her there.

CHAPTER 14

Would Jack the Ripper Be Caught Today?

Jack the Ripper was operating at a time in history when a person could quite literally get away with murder due to the lack of policing techniques that we take for granted today. That's not to discredit the police of that epoch in any way, because they did the best they could with the tools available to them at that time, just as the police force do today – one can only imagine what will be at the disposal to the police in 136 years from now, and our current technology will no doubt look very tame to a future PC. But would the Ripper get away with these crimes today? There isn't any reason why he couldn't, but it would certainly be a much harder task. People will claim that the London East End of 1888 was a very different one compared to today, and this, of course, is true. Time moves on and places change, long gone are the days of a mostly working class area that was very much being driven by poverty despite the status of London within the British Empire. It is also very easy to wear rose-tinted glasses when thinking of Victorian London, the fog, the gloom, the rain, muddy, stinking streets, poor sewage, run-down housing, people clad in old, dirty, torn clothes, and even Jack the Ripper is seen as a tall, dark and handsome man dressed in the finest clothes with top hat and cloak. Of course, you must remember that this could not be because this would obviously draw much unwanted attention to the killer, so the complete opposite is more likely the case as he'd very much want to blend in with the average man on the street. This is where Lechmere could fit in so perfectly because he was a working-class man who worked as a Victorian equivalent of a modern-day white van man at a meat processing factory. He would be covered in blood as part of his work and so could slip in and out of the crowds with relevant ease with no question. News of the Ripper killings would have been spread by word of mouth or via newspapers. Newspapers were a fast growing industry, they would print several editions a day and would often sensationalise the news just to secure the extra sales. Of the Ripper killings, graphic accounts were delivered to the worried populations, along with witness accounts and sketched artistic impressions were drawn. Today, of course, it would be very different. People have mobile phones in their pockets with high quality cameras that are ready in an instant to record images or video, and with social media, these images can be viewed by people around the world within seconds. Newspapers are still circulating, and though definitely not the force they once were, they still reach a considerable audience with their circulations. TV crews can be at the scene of a crime in moments, before broadcasting the reports and pictures worldwide in minutes. There is literally no hiding place when it comes to the media once they are set on a subject. What of CCTV? This is very probably the single reason why the Ripper would be caught today. London alone has over half a million CCTV cameras, which is no doubt an underestimation, with people having cameras in their cars, doorbells etc. Being able to avoid any one of these would today be nigh on impossible unless the Ripper could plan an almost impossible route around these things. The quality of the cameras has moved on with technology too, no longer are many cameras grainy; they are HD ready, and would easily detect any killer or criminal.

Photography of the scene of a crime has obviously changed hugely over the years too. At a crime scene today, the police will arrive, before proceeding to tape off the area and, if a body is on site, a tent will be placed around the body until the forensic teams arrive and collect all available evidence before the body is finally released to the coroner. If we remember the murder of Annie Chapman on 8 September 1888, there was no privacy for the poor woman because poverty-stricken people living in the area overlooking the body would sell time for people to gaze down upon her, and such a volume of people would quickly destroy all evidence.

What of DNA evidence? The attacks were savage beyond belief and there can be absolutely no way that DNA evidence wasn't left behind. That said, had the evidence gathering and testing been as good as it is today, the letters and postcard sent could have been tested, as well as all important pieces of evidence like Catherine Eddowes' shawl. Without a shadow of doubt, that shawl contained DNA evidence from the Ripper. Sadly, because of the age of the shawl and the countless people it has been in contact with, all original DNA has been destroyed beyond recognition. So, all this in mind, the Ripper could possibly have succeeded in his fantasies if he modified his ways, but in truth, the chances of it being an unsolved mystery for 136 years are slim. Nothing is impossible but one wouldn't wish to take the pitiful odds a bookmaker would give over him being caught and convicted. The Ripper lived in an age where, as long as a plan was conceived and meticulously planned, one could get away with murder. That said, the Ripper was almost caught on at least two occasions either because he became arrogant or because his bloodlust compulsion overtook him, a combination of the two factors is probably the cause.

All being said and done, the identity of Jack the Ripper will forever be a mystery in that no full conclusive proof to his identity will ever come forward. That said, I believe that the killer was hiding in plain sight all along and his name was Charles Allen Lechmere/Cross.

Bibliography

Books

Begg, Paul, *Jack the Ripper: CSI – Whitechapel*, Andre Deutsch Limited, London, 2012

Begg, Paul, *Jack the Ripper: The Facts*, Robson Books Limited, London, 2006

Begg, Paul, *Jack the Ripper: The Uncensored Facts*, Robson Books Limited, London, (1988) 1990

Berry, James, *My Experiences As An Executioner by Ernest A. Parr*, Percy Lund, Humphries & Co., Bradford, 1892

Cornwell, Patricia, *Portrait of A Killer: Jack the Ripper – Case Closed*, Little, Brown Book Group Limited, London, 2002

Dew, Walter, *I Caught Crippen: Memoirs of Ex-Chief Inspector Walter Dew, CID*, Blackie & Son, Glasgow, 1938

Doyle, Arthur Conan, *A Study in Scarlet*, Ward, Lock & Co., London, 1887

Doyle, Arthur Conan, *The Adventures of Sherlock Holmes*, George Newnes Limited, London, 1892

Doyle, Arthur Conan, *The Sign of the Four*, Lippincott's, London, 1890

Evans, Stewart P. and Gainey, *Jack the Ripper: First American Serial Killer*, Kodansha, United States, 1996

Evans, Stewart P. and Rumbelow, Donald, *Jack the Ripper: Scotland Yard Investigates*, The History Press, Gloucestershire, 2006

Evans, Stewart P. and Skinner, Keith, Stewart, *Jack the Ripper Letters: From Hell*, The History Press, Gloucestershire, (1994) 2001

Bibliography

Evans, Stewart P. and Skinner, Keith, *The Ultimate Jack The Ripper Sourcebook*, Robinson, London (2000) 2001

Fairclough, Melvyn, *The Ripper and the Royals*, Gerard Duckworth & Co., London, 1992

Hinton, Bob, *From Hell: The Jack The Ripper Mystery*, Old Bakehouse Publications, United Kingdom, (1998) 2005

Holmgren, Christer, *Cutting Point, Solving the Jack the Ripper and the Thames Torso Murders*, Timaios Press, Sweden, 2021

Jullian, Philippe, *Édouard VII*, Hachette, London, 1962

Keogh, Steven, *Murder Investigation Team: How Killers Are Really Caught...*, John Blake, London, (2022) 2023

Marriott, Trevor, *Jack the Ripper: The 21st Century Investigation*, John Blake, London, 2007

Smith, Henry, *From Constable to Commissioner: The Story of Sixty Years Most of Them Misspent*, Chatto & Windus, London, 1910

Sugden, Philip, The Complete History of Jack The Ripper, Robinson, London, (1994) 2006

Trow, M.J., *The Thames Torso Murders*, Pen & Sword Books Limited, Barnsley, 2011

Williams, Tony with Price, Humphrey, *Uncle Jack*, The Orion Publishing Group, London, 2005

Interviews

Hutchinson, Melvyn (interviewee) and Fairclough, Melvyn (interviewer) for research for his book, *The Ripper and the Royals*

Magazine Articles

Anderson, Robert, 'The Lighter Side of My Official Life', *Blackwood's Magazine*, Edinburgh, 1910

Stowell, Dr Thomas, 'Prince Albert Victor', *The Criminologist*, 1970

Newspaper Articles

'Coles, Frances', *East London Advertiser*, 14 February 1891
'Coles, Frances', *The Times*, 17 February 1891
'Montague, John Druitt', *Acton, Chiswick & Turnham Green Gazette*, 5 January 1889
'Stride, Elizabeth', *Lloyd's Weekly*, 7 October 1888
'Tabram, Martha', *East London Observer*, 25 August 1888
'Tabram, Martha', *South Wales Echo*, 20 August 1888

Newspapers

Acton, Chiswick & Turnham Green Gazette
Daily Chronicle
East London Advertiser
East London Observer
Financial Times
Liverpool Post
Lloyd's Weekly
South Wales Echo
The Daily News
The Daily Telegraph
The Dundee Courier & Argus
The Herald
The New York Times
The Pall Mall Gazette
The Police Gazette
The Star
The Times
Western Times
Westminster & Pimlico News
Williamsport Sunday Grit

Bibliography

Online Sources

Casebook: Jack the Ripper
  https://forum.casebook.org
Jack the Ripper 1888
  https://www.jack-the-ripper.org
Jack the Ripper Forums
  https://www/jtrforums.com
Jones, Richard, The Jack the Ripper Files, 2015

You Tube
  Blomer, Steve E., Inside Bucks Row, 2023
  Keogh, Steven, Murder Investigation Team: Jack the Ripper A 21st Century Investigation, 2023
    Stow, Edward, House of Lechmere

Wikipedia
  Jack the Ripper Forum (Wikipedia)
  https://en.wikipedia.org (Jack the Ripper)

Records

London Public Asylum

Reference Sources

Bell, Quentin, Biographer
Douglas, John, FBI Profiler (published 1988)
Harrison, Michael, Writer (published 1972)
Hazelwood, Roy, FBI Profiler (published 1988)
Fido, Martin, Ripperologist (published 1987)
Madsen, Diane, Author
Stowell, Thomas E.A., Researcher (published 1970)

Other Books by Author

The Peasenhall Murder: An Edwardian Mystery

Coming Soon

*Hollywood's First Scandal:
The Life and Crime of Roscoe Conkling 'Fatty' Arbuckle*

Index

Abberline, Inspector Frederick George, 64, 67–9, 87, 101, 142
Albert Victor, Prince, 70, 91–2, 105–107
Albrook, Lizzie, 61–2
Aldgate High Street, 48, 54, 146–7
Anderson, Sir Robert, 64, 76, 79, 95–7, 112, 123, 142
Andrews, Police Constable Walter, 111–13
Arnold, Superintendent Thomas, 64, 69

Baker's Row, 23, 136, 138–9
Barnett, Joseph, 59–61, 64, 67, 70, 83–5, 149
Baxter, Wynne Edwin, 7–8, 24, 27, 32, 35, 43–4, 110, 121, 142
Beck, Inspector Walter, 63–4, 68
Bell, Dr Joseph, 105
Bell Court, 46
Berner Street, 40, 53, 114, 123–5, 142, 146
Bethnal Green, 135
Birmingham, 46
Bishopsgate Police Station, 48, 54, 146
Black Lion Yard, 97
Blackwell, Dr Frederick William, 41–2, 44

Bond, Dr Thomas, 53, 64–6, 69, 112, 123, 126
Bostock, Elizabeth, 133
Bowyer, Thomas, 63, 67
Brick Lane, 7–8, 22, 47, 60
Britannia Public House, 30
Broad Street, 135, 146
Brown, Frederick Gordon, 50–1, 53–4, 58
Buck's Row, 23, 26–7, 115, 123–4, 132, 135–40
Bury, William Henry, 70, 92–5
Byfield, Sergeant James, 146–7

Cadosch, Albert, 31
Campbell, Donald, 120
Chandler, Inspector Joseph Luniss, 32
Chapman, Annie, 29–37, 41, 69, 74, 85–6, 114, 141–3, 150, 152
Chapman, George, 70, 85–8
Chapman, John James, 29
Chelsea, 47, 59
Cheltenham, 48
Church Passage, 49–50, 54, 147
City of London
  Cemetery, 28, 58
  Mortuary, 53
  police, 50, 55

Cohen, David, 70, 95–7
Coles, Frances, 116–122
Collard, Inspector, 53
Commercial Road, 10
Commercial Street, 32, 40, 60, 99–100, 102–103, 119, 145, 150
    police station, 12–13, 63, 67, 100
Connelly, Mary Ann 'Pearly Poll', 10–11, 13–17
Conway, Thomas, 46–7
Cooper, Eliza, 30, 33
Cox, Mary Ann, 62–3, 67–8
Cream, Dr Thomas Neill, 70, 89–91
Cross, Charles Allen, *see* Lechmere, Charles Allen
Crossingham's Lodging House, 30
Cutbush, Thomas Hayne, 70, 97

Davis, John, 31–2
Dew, DC Walter, 6, 8, 17
Dimmock, Emily, 77
DNA, 78, 153
Donovan, Timothy, 30, 32–3
Dorset Street, 5, 30, 47, 60–2, 64, 68, 101–102, 116, 123–5, 144
Douglas, John, 128–9
Doyle, Arthur Conan, 105
Druitt, Montague John, 70–4, 80, 107
Duke Street, 49–50, 147
Dutfield's Yard, 40, 45, 142

East End, 1, 47, 60, 87, 110, 127, 151
East India Dock Road, 38
East London Cemetery, 45
Eddowes, Catherine, 46–51, 53, 58, 69, 85, 127, 142–3, 146–9, 153

Farquharson, 73
Farrant Street, 6
Foster, Elizabeth, 53, 62

George Yard, 11–12, 17, 87
Golden Jubilee, 1
Golden Lane Mortuary, 53–4, 58
Goulston Street, 50, 55–6, 127, 148

Halse, Detective Constable Daniel, 55
Hammersmith, 72
Hanbury Street, 23, 31–3, 85, 110, 123–4, 136, 139, 141–2, 150
Harvey, PC James, 50, 54
Haslip, George, 7–8
Hayes, Margaret, 6
Hazelwood, Roy, 128
Helson, Inspector Joseph, 26
Holland, PC, 50
Hutchinson, George, 62–3, 70, 100–104
Hutt, PC George, 49, 146–7

Imperial Club, 49
International Working Men's Educational Club, 40, 43

Kaminsky, Nathan, *see* David Cohen
Kelly, James, 70, 98
Kelly, John, 47–8, 53, 55, 58
Kelly, John (Mary Jane Kelly's father), 59
Kelly, Mary Jane, 59–69, 82–5, 98–103, 116, 123, 127–8, 130–1, 142–3, 147–9
Kent, 47–8, 88
Kidney, Michael, 39, 44, 143–5
Killeen, Dr, 12–13, 17

Index

Klosowski, Seweryn Antonowicz, *see* Chapman, George
Knightsbridge, 29
Kosminski, Aaron, 70, 74–6, 95–7

Lambeth Workhouse, 19–21, 24
Lawende, 49, 54, 147
Lechmere, Charles, Allen, 23–6, 70, 104, 132–41, 143, 146, 148, 150, 153
Limerick, 59
Littlechild, Chief Inspector John, 79–81
Llewellyn, Dr, 23–5, 27, 137
London Metropolitan Police, 75
Long, PC Alfred, 50, 55
Long, Elizabeth, 31
Lusk, George, 56–8, 85
  Lusk Letter, 56–7

Macnaghten, Sir Melville, 73, 75, 89, 95, 142
Manor Park Cemetery, 36
Maybrick, James, 70, 81–3
McCarthy, John, 61, 63–4, 67
McKenzie, Alice, 110–12, 114
McWilliam, Detective Inspector James, 55
Mile End,
  Casual Ward, 48
  Old Town Workhouse, 75
Mile End Road, 57
Miller's Court, 60–4, 67–8, 84–5, 101–102, 115, 149–50
Mitre Square, 49–50, 53–4, 123, 147–8
Mizen, PC Jonas, 23–4, 26, 136–40
Monk, Mary Ann, 21, 24, 27

Monro, Chief Commissioner James, 108–109, 112, 114–16
Montague Street Mortuary, 27
Mylett, Rose, 108–110

Neil, PC John, 23–5, 27, 135–7, 139–40
Nichols, Mary Ann 'Polly', 19–28, 32, 35–6, 69, 74, 132, 135–7, 139–43
Nichols, William, 19–20, 26
Notting Hill, 30

Old Montague Street Mortuary, 24
Openshaw, Dr Thomas Horrocks, 57, 78
Osborn Street, 7, 22, 27
Ostrog, Michael, 70, 88–9

Paul, Robert, 23, 26, 136–7, 139
Pavilion Yard Mortuary, 25
Phillips, Dr George Bagster, 32, 41–2, 44, 47, 52, 54, 63–4, 66, 68, 112, 117, 141–2
Pinchin Street, 114–16, 133–4
Pizer, John, 36
Prater, Elizabeth, 62–3, 68
Princess Alice (pub), 119
Princess Alice, SS, 39, 44, 145
Poplar, 39, 108, 145
  Workhouse, 39

Queen's Head (pub), 40, 101
Queen Victoria, 1, 5, 91

Reid, Inspector Edmund, 7–8, 12–15, 64, 67, 145
Richardson, John, 31, 33, 35
Robinson, PC Louis Frederick, 48, 146

Sadler, James Thomas, 119–22
Saunders, William, 53–4, 58
Schwartz, Israel, 43, 143
Scotland Yard, 37, 64, 73, 96, 105
Sequeira, George William, 50, 53–4
Sickert, Walter, 70, 76–9
Simmons, PC George, 48, 146
Sims, George, 79–81
Smith, Eliza Ann, *see* Chapman, Annie
Smith, Emma Elizabeth, 6–8, 17
Smith, Major Henry, 58
Smith, PC William, 40, 142–3
Southwark, 9, 19
Spitalfields, 7, 36, 68, 102, 113, 129, 133
   Dorset Street, 60, 144
   Flower and Dean Street, 22, 39–40, 47
   George Street, 10
   Gun Street, 110
   Thrawl Street, 22, 60
Spitalfields Market, 31
Spratling, Inspector, 24, 26
St James's Place, 56
Stephen, James Kenneth, 105–107
Stride, Elizabeth, 38–45, 53, 56, 69, 103, 142–4, 146
Swanson, Chief Inspector Donald Sutherland, 58, 76, 79, 95–6, 115, 120, 142
Sweden, 38

Tabram, Charles, 9–10
Tabram, Henry, 16
Tabram, Martha, 9–13, 16–17, 28, 142–3
Tanner, Elizabeth, 40, 44
Ten Bells (pub), 62–3
Thain, PC John, 23, 27
Thames, River, 9, 39, 72–3, 83
Thames Magistrates' Court, 36
Thicke, Sergeant William, 36
Thompson, Police Constable Ernest, 116–17
Tumblety, Dr Francis, 70, 79–81
Turner, William, 9–10, 16

Victoria Home for Working Men, 100, 103

Wandsworth, 21
   Prison, 87
Warren, Sir Charles, 3–4, 20, 50, 112
Watkins, PC Edward, 49, 53–4, 147
Whitechapel, *passim*
   Union Workhouse, 10
Whitechapel Mortuary, 12, 36
Whitechapel Road, 13, 22–4, 27, 45, 135
White Swan pub, 10
Wiles, Dr Frederick, 57
Williams, Sir John, 70, 99–100
Winthrop Street, 135
Wolverhampton, 46, 93
Working Lad's Institute, 13, 16, 24, 32